The
Gospel
according to
Mary

✦

An imaginative work

The Gospel according to Mary

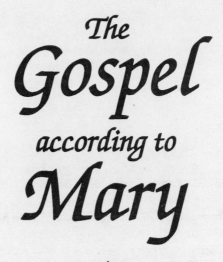

❖

A New Testament for Women

❖❖❖

MIRIAM THERESE WINTER

CROSSROAD · NEW YORK

1993

The Crossroad Publishing Company
370 Lexington Avenue, New York, NY 10017

Copyright © 1993 by the Medical Mission Sisters

Printed in the United States of America

Library of Congress Cataloging-in-Publication Data
Winter, Miriam Therese.
    The gospel according to Mary : a New Testament for women /
Miriam Therese Winter
        p. cm.
    ISBN 0-8245-1174-3 (pbk.)
    1. Jesus Christ—Biography. 2. Feminist theology. I. Gospel
according to Mary. II. Title.
BT301.2.W54 1993
232.9'01—dc20   92-40353
                                                           CIP

CONTENTS

✦

INTRODUCTION

✦

It must be said, right at the beginning, that *The Gospel According to Mary* is an imaginative work. Imaginative, but not ahistoric, for this text, which is not entirely factual, is not exactly fiction. It is essentially the story of Jesus, the good news of his life lived before and after dying.

This gospel makes explicit what might have been and still is of primary interest to women and hints at the development of a women's tradition which differed from that of the men. It may help us to see more clearly how Jesus entrusted to women the essentials of our Christian faith, how women were not only present in all of the important places, but were keepers of the vision, even when, time after time, no one else believed them. Women were the continuity spanning the before and after of the advent of the Living God; women were central to the birth of Jesus, witnesses to his death and to his resurrection, and present at Pentecost. Their constancy is evident from the canonical accounts, as is the pattern of betrayal, disbelief, denial, and desertion of the men.

This gospel was written by a woman for women and for others who feel excluded and for all who feel unsatisfied with the traditional understanding of the foundations of Christian life. It offers another way of looking at Jesus and tradition, and it does so in order that we might stop and think, and reflect, and ask pointed questions, and

15

then look to one another for answers, trusting that as we search together and share faith formed through our diverse experience, God's Spirit will speak through us. Only a new perspective shared by women and men together will foster the conviction necessary for broad-based social change. May this text, with its necessarily limited view, serve as a stepping stone toward a more enlightened understanding of that radically inclusive Gospel born of God's Wisdom and God's Word.

I invite you to join with me in exploring a dimension of a tradition we think we know. We will imagine as we remember, turn the familiar upside down, move outside the lines. As an alternative to intellectual exploration, imagine how the good news proclaimed to and through women might witness to a new world order which many today are convinced that Jesus sought to bring about.

The Gospel According to Mary is meant as a resource for a spirituality already present in many women and men. Its purpose is to lift the good news up to God and to ask Her to say it again. It is a plea on behalf of women: tell us in our own words about Your Word made flesh among us, Your Word enfleshed in us. It is a prayer from the depths of women's spirit: come, Wellspring of Wisdom, source of our own intuitive wisdom. Come and make all things new.

The Twentieth-Century Writer and Her Perspectives

If I were intent on adhering to the precepts of scriptural scholarship, I would not have written this book. The discipline of New Testament studies has principles and rules. A feminist critique and reconstruction must follow a sound methodology and move forward step by step. This book, however, is not academic, nor strictly speaking, biblical. Although traditional interpretation and some well-founded assumptions form part of the manuscript, it arises from a world of make-believe and "once upon a time" where it weaves both facts and fantasy into a web of "let's pretend." Some will say I have gone too far, others, not far enough. Still others will be startled by the gospel format and use of scriptural texts.

I wrote *The Gospel According to Mary* out of a context of creative freedom and a deep inner conviction that what I was doing needed to be done. I will not blame the biblical women and say they made me do it, but I can honestly say that, as I wrote, their spirits were hovering near. Imaginative, intuitive writing comes from that place where dreams come from and to which the heart returns, a place that gives us songs and psalms, poetry and prayer, and permission to break the rules. As in dreams, one can mix metaphors, be lyrical instead of literal, wishful, or whimsical, even inappropriate.

While the method of appropriation and a good deal of the content flow from the imagination, the scriptures as we know them were my basic starting point. I used the four canonical gospels as primary source material and kept as close as possible to what I call the gospel feeling. I wanted to create a resource one would recognize as gospel and perhaps use in alternative rituals or privately for prayer. That meant a style and format which would replicate the original. I decided to build on traditional narratives, parables, and sayings, and to retain familiar passages where I thought it felt right to do so. This was no small decision. I knew I would be doing a delicate dance through a minefield of public opinion, prime target for those for whom scripture was God's literal word and forever sacrosanct; and for those who, for reasons too numerous to name, would cringe at the merging of four distinct gospels with their complex textual traditions or would simply feel irreverent reading this reworking of sacred texts; and for those for whom the biblical texts and even biblical tradition are no longer relevant. Then for whom have I written this gospel? For people like me, I guess, women who want to continue to experience the transformative power of God's word and its culturally conditioned truth inherent in authoritative, androcentric scriptures. As a lifelong lover of the biblical word and rooted in biblical tradition, I want what was meaningful to me in the past to continue to be meaningful now, not only as an occasional path but as an avenue into Life. Out of fidelity to the Spirit, I conceived *The Gospel According to Mary* as a resource for personal piety and a context for a collective response to the word that lives in us.

This gospel has two distinct parts, one which functions as historical narrative focusing on the life and mission of Jesus, the other an anthology of his teachings. The anthology interrupts the narrative with four self-contained chapters of parables and selected sayings organized by topic or theme. The first half of the narrative moves through the early life of Jesus, his call to mission and ministry, and a compilation of his miracles. The second half begins with texts related to Jesus' own self-identification followed by texts about discipleship. It culminates in his death and resurrection and the outpouring of his Spirit.

Some of the more challenging myths or legends concerning the birth and resurrection of Jesus and some aspects of his ministry have been left more or less intact, and the syllabus of sayings makes no attempt to distinguish between his actual words and what others may have said he said. This is an apocryphal gospel, therefore much liberty has been taken in what is recorded here.

Some traditional material has been included. Much has been left out. What is included has been reinterpreted. The rewording of various episodes is clearly an invitation to engage one's imagination and to confront one's prejudice. For example, it is suggested that Elizabeth the wife of Zechariah may not necessarily be the one responsible for the couple's childlessness. The sister of Mary whom we encounter in John's Gospel standing at the foot of the cross is Mary's lifelong companion, the first to hear the astonishing news of her sister's pregnancy. The episode of the Magi, long thought to be apocryphal, focuses on the women, a departure from the original text. Material from the Gnostic gospels defines Mary Magdalene and her discipleship role. The implicit presence of women is made explicit throughout the gospel. For example, with Jairus's daughter, after Jesus restores the little girl to life, she gets up and runs to her mother. In this gospel women are prominent, not an afterthought. When taken all together, these changes yield a text which testifies to the preeminence of women. Even if it is only imaginary, it feels good for a change.

A distinct characteristic of *The Gospel According to Mary* is that all of the parables included here are gender-specific for women. That is not so very radical. Parables are figurative, metaphoric, which means they are far more effective when indigenous to a group. A gender enculturation should make the parables more accessible to women, and that really is good news.

The Gospel According to Mary is intent on telling the story of Jesus uninterrupted by "thealogical" discourse. Nevertheless, my own thealogical perspective, and the experience and concerns of women today, played a part in shaping the text. Some of the underlying assumptions were influenced by feminist scholarship, others by the lived reality of women-church and our global sisterhood. Among these assumptions are the following.

Women were active participants in the mission and ministry of Jesus. This fundamental assumption is reflected in the text. Women were among the disciples of Jesus, and it is more than likely that there was no distinction between apostles and disciples. Women and men shared leadership in the apostolic church because of the example of Jesus, who redefined leadership roles.

A women's culture is emerging today, and it is slowly being integrated into the message and meaning of Jesus as it is translated into images and symbols in our rituals and our songs. We women want to hand this tradition down to our daughters and our granddaughters and to share it with female friends. We long for it to be rooted in the wider canonical tradition and continue to search for linkages to our sisters in the past.

Women today are far more intuitive in interpreting tradition, less linear, less literal, less legal. Many feel free to depart from the lections or to adapt text to context when scripture is proclaimed. Fairly comfortable with metaphor and story, with poetry and parable, with an embodied literacy, we tend to take the point of a narrative and retell it in our own way. We are wary of patriarchal expectations, and consequently find we are often faced with a liturgy of scarcity. Our intuition tells us that women of early Christianity have something to say to us here.

We women try to support one another as we struggle to overcome the social separations dictated by culture and class, the prejudice of race and gender, the distinctions of age and status, of lineage and wealth. We wonder if women in the life of Jesus felt the same way we do, and if they carried this spirit of solidarity into the apostolic church.

As women we are inclined to remember the experiences of other women. We are affected by moments that touch or transform women's lives. Today we are making an effort to lift women from anonymity to visibility, from the margins to the center, and we want to see ourselves, our gender, reflected in our scripture and our celebrational texts.

Women today want a scripture that does not disadvantage any living thing, that avoids making negative comparisons or alluding to a hierarchy of good, better, best.

Women look to a Jesus who is warm and sensitive and human, who stands in the strength of an inner truth and speaks with authority. We identify with his compassion for people, love for the earth, awareness of all creation. We want to proclaim that radical gospel of genuine inclusiveness, affirmation and empowerment of women, predilection for the marginated and oppressed, uncompromising commitment to a mission of justice and peace. We are convinced that these qualities, these gospel values, must characterize the contemporary church. Hierarchy, primacy, triumphalism, excessive regulation, prejudice, exclusion, violence and war, destruction of the earth's resources, indifference to the suffering of people have nothing to do with Jesus. As church, we have often violated others in memory of him.

Feminist theologians and biblical scholars are questioning the revelatory nature of traditional canonical texts which consistently exclude women and discount women's experience. They claim that the latter-day context in which the word is proclaimed to us is just as important as the original context in which it first arose. If the biblical word is not liberating for women, it is not God's life-giving word. *The Gospel According to Mary* takes women seriously by looking to feminist contexts for interpretation and validation, urging us all to envision what the just church might look like and how it might function as sacrament in the midst of a wounded world. This hermeneutical method lies at the heart of this imaginary gospel and is basically the reason why this resource came to be.

Precedent for understanding that the word of God transcends any written word lies within the tradition. Retelling God's word in human words was the task for generations of biblical liturgy. Many of our Gospel narratives arose out of or were shaped by liturgical traditions. That means that the scriptures transmitting them to us convey the word of God along with the wisdom and opinions of diverse communities struggling to construct a way of life from their memories of Jesus and a variety of interpretive guides. Reflecting separate traditions, they tell us that we too are to be actively engaged in the search for meaning, that the gospel word is a living word that must live again in us. Even as the canonical scriptures remain the authoritative source of Christian revelation, it is important to recognize that God reveals Godself to us in every aspect of life. Before there was a book God is and has already acted, for behind the biblical texts lies a lengthy oral tradition which, like our own, once it has passed, can never be recalled and may never be recognized.

The Gospel According to Mary affirms that a primary source of revelation is in the world around us and in the wisdom deep within us, where the Spirit of the living God continues to make all things new. It locates our contemporary struggles at the heart of our biblical tradition and links our complex everyday lives to all that has gone before. This is the task of the liturgy, to help us make the connections between the word spoken through tradition and the word enfleshed in our lives. The task of feminist liturgy is to tell us over and over again to trust our experience which is where God's wisdom resides. To depart from scripture momentarily is to remain liturgically authentic and indeed biblically based. *The Gospel According to Mary* is a resource for feminist liturgy. What matters is not the text itself but the reflections and shared experience of those who hunger to know and make known the word and wisdom of God.

Let me introduce to you now the co-author of this gospel, my first-century imaginary friend. Through an intuitive collaboration centered somewhere between her world of the past and my world in the present, her effort to remember and mine to envision converged and gave birth to this text. Whether what she remembers is fact or fiction is not really the issue, for the entire work is fantasy. She herself is fantasy. Please remember that.

Now explanation ceases and imagination begins. Set

your imagination free as you read the remaining pages. And every time you read this gospel, trust your intuition and dare to be imaginative, for intuition is the womb of Her wisdom and imagination the cradle of Her word.

The First-Century Writer and Her Sources *Imaginary*

The writer of *The Gospel According to Mary* was the granddaughter of Mary the mother of John Mark, who led a house church in Jerusalem. Her name was also Mary. As a young girl she often went with her mother to worship at her grandmother's house.

Among this first-century writer's sources were her grandmother and three other women named Mary: Mary the mother of Jesus, Mary of Bethany, and Mary Magdalene.

The writer's other sources were women who had been transformed by Jesus, some of whom had been his disciples; women who had been touched by the Spirit on hearing ordinary women like themselves preach at Pentecost; women within and beyond the borders of Judea and Galilee; women of other cultures in community with women, or in communities of women and men.

This woman-source or wisdom-source had a rich oral tradition. In fact, different traditions emerged and developed among the women. One of these spoke of a scandal associated with Mary's first pregnancy, and said that her son was illegitimate, but the writer rejected such views. It was rumored that the sister of the mother of Jesus had kept a diary, but by the time the writer began her gospel, the text could no longer be found. This multifaceted female source we now know as **W**, which stands for **Women** and **Wisdom.** This **W** source functioned for the writer in the manner of the cryptic **Q** in the shaping of the synoptic accounts.

The writer was ten years old during the happenings in Jerusalem. As long as she lived she would never forget the agonized cries of her mother as they stood together on a crowded street and saw that kind and gentle man carrying a wooden cross. He had stopped and spoken directly to them, and all these decades later, she could still feel his presence, still hear his compassionate voice. She was present when the community felt the outpouring of the Spirit, and was there with her mother from the very first moment her grandmother's group was formed. As a little girl she did not understand the meaning of resurrection, but she loved to listen to her grandmother, her mother, and her uncle John Mark reflecting on new beginnings with her family and their friends. Their stories filled her with wonder. She especially loved the singing, and she joined in their prayers of praise.

Mary spent a lot of time with Rhoda, her grandmother's maid. As she sat on a stool in the kitchen, she learned a lot about what went on in many of the other households. Rhoda seemed to know everything, and the two became lifelong friends. Once the mother of Jesus came to pray at her grandmother's house. The other women were often there and she knew them all by name. She was especially drawn to her namesakes and intrigued by the tales they told.

Mary grew up to imitate her grandmother in the breaking of the bread. Her collective memories and childhood experiences were formative and lasting. She drew heavily upon them in the writing of her gospel account.

Mary wrote her gospel toward the close of the first century. She was one of the last females still presiding over a house church by the time she completed her text. Precisely where this was remains unknown. She was revered for her wisdom, which was said to be inspired.

She was a protégée of John, the son of her mother's friend, Salome, who had once been close to Jesus. She had recently received a letter from a member of their circle which outlined some concerns. Her correspondent had addressed her as "Elect Lady" in defiance of the anti-female movement rampant among many males. Mary knew that gospels were already circulating which reflected the bias of men. This shift in ethos and attitude had prompted her to begin writing a gospel of her own.

Mary had witnessed many changes in the apostolic church. The liberating spirit of Jesus which had so energized both women and men and had shaped those earlier communities had been stifled, bit by bit, until a pattern of restrictive practices had redefined the movement along more conservative lines. The church, now an institution, no longer looked kindly on innovation or the informality of women's ways. There was a lot of pressure to make everything everywhere the same. Jewish males continued to assume that the church was the new Jerusalem and had already begun to pattern its praxis according to certain norms.

The church was being buffeted by persecution inside and out. Communities gathered in secret to avoid detection by the authorities, and this need for secrecy had an undermining influence on all aspects of the church. Heretical trends threatened the integrity of the tradition which had been handed down. Circulating letters held warnings. Some epistles were treated as though they had come directly from God. Preaching was more and more proscriptive. The good news entrusted to the next generation was losing its creative edge. There was even talk of a canon, of making certain traditions authoritative for all.

Women everywhere were disheartened. Their leadership was no longer recognized. Their experience was being misinterpreted. Their preaching, teaching, and prophesying had been disqualified on theoretical grounds. What had become of the *koinonia,* that spirit of equality which was the special charism of the Pentecostal church? There were signs that there would soon be a hierarchically divided communion of saints, a church of the elite in which women were sure to feel oppressed. Was it the end of the age of freedom? Would wisdom disappear in the heat of theological definition? Soon no one would remember how it once had been. Women had not yet forgotten, but they had to make sure that the future did not misunderstand their spirited past.

After Mary had finished her gospel, it was circulated surreptitiously and eventually disappeared. Late in the twentieth century, a shepherd girl found the scroll while playing with her sister. It is reproduced here in its entirety, along with a hymn to Wisdom, which may have been an early first-century hymn.

The
Gospel
according to
Mary

✦

Imaginary

In the beginning,
Wisdom:
with God,
within God
eternally.
From the beginning,
Wisdom
is God.

Through Her
all life
came to be,
born of Her light
and Her darkness
and Her rich diversity.

Into the midst of Her world,
She came,
mingled among Her own.
She came,
calling us by name.
She came
to those who would receive Her.

Wisdom
made flesh
Her dwelling place,
gives
from Her fullness
grace
upon grace,
intuitively
lives
in the hollow space
within
as in
the beginning.

GOD'S WORD
TO AND THROUGH WOMEN

Because others have written of the events that have taken place among us, proclaiming according to their own understanding the good news handed down by those who were eye-witnesses to the ministry of Jesus, I too have decided to write an account so that women might know of the experiences of women from the beginning until now.

ELIZABETH AND MARY

✧

Elizabeth

During the days when Herod was king of Judea and men alone were responsible for the things that pertained to God, there lived a holy woman whose priestly lineage went all the way back to Elisheba and Aaron. Her name was Elizabeth. Her husband belonged to the Abijah line of the traditional priesthood, and his name was Zechariah. Both of them lived blamelessly, keeping all the commandments and ordinances faithfully before God. Elizabeth had never had children. Men, assuming that she was at fault, referred to her as barren, while women had long been aware of Zechariah's periodic impotence. They had been married a very long time, and now Elizabeth was beyond her child-bearing years.

One day as Zechariah was leaving to fulfill his priestly office, Elizabeth heard a voice deep within her say, "Elizabeth, be at peace, for the prayer of your heart has been heard. You and Zechariah will have a child, and you are to name him John. You will know the joys of motherhood and your heart will sing with gladness, for many will rejoice at his birth. Your child will be filled with the Spirit while he is still in your womb, for the one you are about to bear will herald a new beginning and prepare the way for God."

Elizabeth ran to her husband. "Blessed be God," she cried aloud. "It must have been an angel who told these things to me." On hearing the words of the messenger of God, Zechariah was astounded. "What foolishness is this?" he asked. "Should I risk ritual defilement on the eve of my priestly duties to do what cannot be done?" Zechariah did not believe her.

Soon after, Zechariah was serving as priest and his section was on duty when it fell to him by lot, according to the custom of the priesthood, to enter the inner sanctuary and offer incense to God. Outside, the people were assembled in prayer. Suddenly, at the side of the altar of incense, Zechariah saw an apparition, and he was terrified. "Do not be afraid, Zechariah. I am Gabriel, sent by God to bring good news to you. Elizabeth's prayer has been heard. She will bear a child. Your son will walk among your people with the spirit and power of Elijah, and he will turn many hearts toward God." Zechariah said to the angel, "How can this be? I am an old man and Elizabeth is no longer young. What am I to do?" The angel replied, "Do whatever Elizabeth tells you. And because you did not believe her, because you dismissed God's word to her, you will be silenced, unable to speak, until these things occur."

Outside the sanctuary the people were waiting, and they wondered at Zechariah's delay. When he appeared, he could not say a word, and they knew he had seen a vision. Zechariah remained among the priests until his service was ended, then returned to his own home.

In due time, Elizabeth conceived. She chose to remain in seclusion, quietly praising God.

Mary

Elizabeth's cousin Mary of Nazareth in Galilee was engaged to a man named Joseph, who was of David's lineage. In the sixth month of Elizabeth's pregnancy, Mary heard a voice that said, "Shalom, favored one! The Spirit of God is with you." A radiant light filled the room. She was frightened and confused. The angelic presence said to her, "Do not be afraid, Mary, for you have found favor with God. You will bear a child, and you will name him Jesus. He will be called God's Child, for he is the one whom God has promised." Mary said, "How can this be, for I am without a husband?" The angel replied, "The Spirit of God will encircle you, and the power of the Most High will enter you. The child to be born will be holy, for he is the child of God. Now your relative Elizabeth, in her old age, has also conceived a child. The one who was said to be barren is already six months pregnant, for nothing is beyond God's power." Then Mary said, "I am fully open to the will of God. Let it happen as you say."

Mary and Elizabeth

Mary reflected on all that had been said to her, reliving the words in her heart. In due time she told her sister, and together they told their mother. It was decided that Mary would go at once to stay with Elizabeth. She could assist her elderly cousin as she prepared for the birth of her child. While she was away, her mother, Anne, would speak to her father; and he would go to Joseph. Perhaps Joachim could convince Joseph, even now, to take Mary as his wife.

Mary, accompanied by her sister and an older relative,

set out for the home of her cousin in the hill country of Judea. Elizabeth was ecstatic when she heard Mary's greeting resounding through her house. Even her baby moved within her. Filled with the Spirit, Elizabeth exclaimed, "Blessed are you among women, and blessed is the child of your womb. Tell me, why should the mother of the one long awaited come to visit me? As soon as I heard your greeting, the child within me leaped for joy. Blessed are you who dared to believe God's promise would be fulfilled." Then Elizabeth joined Mary in a canticle of praise.

"My soul proclaims the power of God,
my spirit delights in Her wonderful ways,
for She has shown favor to me, a woman.
Generations of women will all be blessed,
for She Who has power to open the womb
has done inconceivable things through me:
Holy is Her Name.
Her mercy flows through mother and child
from generation to generation.
She silences the arrogant
with the strength of Her outstretched arm,
puts down principalities and powers
as She empowers the poor,
feeds those who are hungry,
while those who seem to have everything
are left unsatisfied.
We have felt Her compassionate presence
as She spoke through our mothers and grandmothers,
keeping the promise She made to Sarah
and her daughters, now and forever."

Mary remained with her cousin until after the birth of Elizabeth's baby.

Birth of Elizabeth's Baby

When the time came for Elizabeth to deliver, she gave birth to a son. Her relatives and friends praised God and rejoiced along with her.

On the eighth day the family gathered for the circumcision of the child. All assumed he would be called Zechariah, which was his father's name, but the baby's mother protested, saying, "He is to be called John." They paid no attention to her. "None of your relatives has this name," they said to Zechariah, the father of the child. He motioned for a writing tablet and wrote, "The mother said, his name is John." Everyone was amazed. Then Zechariah's voice returned to him and he spoke, praising God. Word spread to the neighboring villages, and people throughout the hill country of Judea talked about these things. "What will this child become?" they asked, "for surely God is with him."

Elizabeth and Zechariah, filled with the Spirit of wisdom and with love for their newborn child, sang a canticle of praise:

"Blessed be God forever,
for She has visited Her people,
liberating us, and through us,
liberating all Her sons and daughters.
We are saved from all who would harm us,
through a covenant of mercy
promised by the prophets,
that we might serve God fearlessly

in holiness and justice
all the days of our life.
You, little child, are the prophet
God has called
to prepare the way,
to proclaim a year of favor
and the forgiveness of our sins,
to reveal God's tender mercy
as a new dawn breaks upon us,
filling with light all those who sit
in the shadow of oppression,
guiding us with integrity
along the paths of peace."

The child grew strong in spirit under the guidance of
Elizabeth and Zechariah until the day he appeared as a
prophet in the wilderness of Judea.

MARY'S CHILD

◇

Birth of Mary's Baby

When Mary returned to Nazareth, it was evident that she was with child. Joseph, a sensitive man, was unwilling to expose her to public disgrace and had decided to dismiss her quietly, for he could not go through with the marriage. Just as he was about to break their engagement, an angel appeared to him in a dream, saying, "Joseph of the lineage of David, do not be afraid to take Mary as your wife, for the child in her is God's child. She will bear a son whose name will be Jesus; he is the one whom God has promised." When Joseph awoke, he changed his plans and did as the angel had commanded. He took Mary as his wife. They agreed to live as brother and sister until after the birth of her child.

As Mary's time for delivery drew near, a decree was issued calling for a census. Mary went with Joseph to his own town where he had to go to be registered. They traveled from Nazareth in Galilee to Bethlehem in Judea, because this was the city of David. While they were there, Mary gave birth to a baby boy. She wrapped him warmly in homespun cloth and laid him in a manger, for there was no room for them in the inn.

In that region shepherds camped out in the fields to watch over their flocks at night. Suddenly a bright light filled the sky, and they heard what sounded like angels, singing,

> "Glory to God on high,
> and on earth,
> peace and good will among all."

The shepherds were terrified yet at the same time some women among them were also filled with a sense of well-being and peace. That feeling returned when they saw the little child lying in one of their mangers. They shared this with the mother who marveled at their expressions of faith and treasured their words in her heart. The shepherds left, loudly praising and glorifying God for all that they had experienced and for all God had revealed to them.

Naming of Mary's Baby

After eight days had passed, Mary's son was circumcised. She called him Jesus, the name which had been revealed to her in Nazareth by an angel.

Jesus Is Presented in the Temple

When the time came for their purification according to the Law of Moses, Mary and Joseph took the child to the temple in Jerusalem, for it is written in the law that every firstborn male is to be consecrated to God. In presenting their child, they offered the customary sacrifice of two young pigeons, as stated in the law.

Witness of Anna

There was a prophet, Anna, the daughter of Phanuel of the tribe of Asher, a widow eighty-four years of age whose husband had died seven years after the day of their marriage. She was living in the temple precincts, completely dedicated to the worship of God through fasting and through prayer. The moment she saw Mary's baby, she began to praise God and to speak of the child to all who had been longing for the liberation of Jerusalem.

Witness of Simeon

Now there lived in Jerusalem a devout man whose name was Simeon. It had been revealed to him that he would not die until he had seen the Messiah. Inspired by the Spirit, he came to the temple, where he saw the child with his mother. Taking the baby into his arms, he praised God aloud, saying,

> "O Holy One of Blessing,
> now I can depart in peace,
> for my own eyes have seen this day
> Your promise of salvation
> which is spoken to all people,
> a light to enlighten unbelievers
> and to reveal Your abiding glory
> to all in Israel."

The child's mother and father were amazed at what was said about him. After blessing them, Simeon said to Mary, "This child of yours is destined for the fall and for the rise of many. He will be a sign that is rejected, so the secret thoughts of many may be openly revealed. And one day in the future, a sword will pierce your soul." When they had finished everything required by law, they returned with Jesus to Galilee, to their own town of Nazareth, to make a home for him.

Sometime after Mary and Joseph had settled down in Nazareth, some women arrived from Jerusalem. They were elders, known for their wisdom, and they had come to warn the young mother Mary of the danger concerning her child. Shepherds from over in Bethlehem were telling tales of a baby boy whom they said had to be the Messiah. They had seen the child, heard angelic hosts, and spoke of a new revelation; and the women had believed them. Others had dismissed their story, but Herod was taking no chances. He was troubled by an unusual star that had appeared recently in the heavens. He took it as a sign. The word was out that he intended to kill all the male children in and around Bethlehem who were two years old or under. Sooner or later he was bound to learn of the birth of Mary's baby; it had been recorded during the census. She had to leave immediately. They had brought her some gold — their bracelets, a few coins — and some frankincense and myrrh, to help her pay for the journey. Together the women mourned for the mothers and all the innocent children who were about to be slaughtered, crying:

> "A voice was heard in Ramah,
> a woman wailing and lamenting,
> Rachel weeping for her children,
> refusing to be comforted,
> because they are no more."

Flight into Egypt

The women tried to convince Joseph of the urgency of the situation. He agreed that their story was frightening, but he did not really believe them. After they left, an angel appeared to Joseph in a dream, saying, "Get up quickly, and take the child and his mother into Egypt; for Herod is about to search for the boy, and he will surely destroy him." Then Joseph got up, and in the middle of the night, he and the child and the baby's mother journeyed down to Egypt, and remained there until Herod died.

Return from Egypt

One day while he was in Egypt, an angel again appeared to Joseph in a dream, saying, "Take the child and his mother and return home, for those who would kill him are dead." Joseph told Mary, and together they took Jesus and went back to Galilee to their home in Nazareth. There the child grew in wisdom and strength, with God's favor fully upon him.

Jesus in the Temple

Now every year Mary and Joseph went up to Jerusalem for the Passover festival, and Jesus accompanied them. They went to the festival as usual when the boy was twelve years old. When all who had journeyed together were ready to return to Galilee, they departed from the city, but Jesus was not among them. He had been left behind in Jerusalem, but his parents did not know it. Assuming he was among the travelers, they went a full day's journey before they started to look for him among their relatives and friends. When they did not find him, they returned to Jerusalem and searched the city for him. After three days, they found him sitting among the teachers in the temple, listening, asking questions. Everyone was amazed at the extent of his understanding. His parents were not impressed. Overcome with anxiety, yet greatly relieved, his mother said to him, "Child, why have you done this to us? Your father and I have looked everywhere for you. We were growing desperate." Surprised, Jesus said to them, "Why were you searching everywhere? Did you not know I would wait here in God's house until you returned for me?" The child was wise beyond his years. They had yet to comprehend this. He went home with them to Nazareth, where he caused them no further concern.

As the years passed, his mother treasured all these experiences in her heart. And Jesus grew in wisdom and age, favored by God, and popular with others. Joseph was a true father to Mary's firstborn and treated the boy no differently than their other sons and daughters. Sometime before Jesus left home to proclaim his gospel throughout Judea, the aging Joseph died.

Wedding at Cana

There was a wedding in Cana in Galilee, of Mary's sister's child, and all the relatives were invited. Jesus arrived from Nazareth with his mother and his sisters and brothers. There were many guests, family and friends, and the festivities were well underway when suddenly the wine ran out. Clearly upset, Mary approached her firstborn and said, "There is no more wine." Jesus knew what she was asking of him. To be sure she understood the implications of her request, he said, "Is this a concern that warrants my acting before my time has come?" She looked at him, then said to the servants, "Do whatever he tells you." Now standing nearby were six stone water jars for the Jewish rites of purification. Each held about twenty or thirty gallons. Jesus said, "Fill the jars with water." And they filled them to the brim. Then he said to them, "Now draw some out and take it to the chief steward for his approval." And they did. When the steward tasted the water made wine, he had no idea where it came from, but the servants knew. The steward then said to those who had planned and prepared for the wedding celebration, "Everyone serves the good wine first, then later, when the guests are more or less drunk, they bring out inferior wine. But you have kept the best wine until now." Jesus did this first sign in Cana for his mother.

PREPARATION FOR MINISTRY

✧

Ministry of John

In the fifteenth year of the reign of Emperor Tiberius, when Pontius Pilate was governor of Judea and Herod ruler of Galilee, when Herod's brother Philip ruled the region of Ituraea and Trachonitis, and Lysanias ruled Abilene, during the high priesthood of Annas and Caiaphas, the word of God came to John, Elizabeth's son, out in the wilderness. He lived there, clothed in camel's skin with a leather belt around his waist, and he survived on locusts and wild honey. He wandered all around the Jordan, proclaiming a baptism of repentance for the forgiveness of sins.

Crowds came to hear him, people from Jerusalem and the Judean countryside. Many saw him as the fulfillment of the words of the prophet Isaiah:

"The voice of one crying in the wilderness:
'Prepare the way of God, make straight the paths.
Every valley shall be filled,
and every mountain and hill shall be made low,
the crooked shall be made straight,
and the rough ways, smooth;
and all flesh shall see the salvation of God.'"

45

Many confessed their sins and were baptized by John in the river Jordan. People asked him, "What should we do?" He said to them, "Whoever among you has two coats must share with the one who has none; and whoever has food must do the same." Tax collectors asked him, "Teacher, what should we do?" He answered, "Collect no more than the amount prescribed." Soldiers also asked him, "And we, what should we do?" He replied, "Do not extort money from anyone by threats or false accusation, and be satisfied with what you are paid."

Now the people were filled with expectation, secretly wondering whether John himself might be the Messiah. He silenced such speculation. "One is coming who is more powerful than I. I am not worthy to carry his sandals, or to untie his sandal thong. I have baptized you with water. He will baptize you with the Spirit of God, and with wisdom, and with fire."

Baptism of Jesus

One day Jesus came from Nazareth in Galilee to his cousin John in the wilderness to be baptized by him in the Jordan. At first, John protested, insisting it would be far more appropriate for his cousin to baptize him. In time, he consented, and he baptized Jesus in the Jordan. As Jesus was coming up out of the water, filled with the Spirit of God, he heard a voice, as if from heaven, saying deep within him, "Beloved, you are so precious to Me!"

Temptations

Jesus left the Jordan filled with the Spirit and was led by the Spirit to spend some time in the wilderness on his own. After forty days of fasting from solid foods, he was severely tempted. "If you are God's Anointed, change these stones into loaves of bread." Resisting the temptation, he prayed, "One does not live by bread alone, but by the word and the will of God." Then it seemed as if he were being transported bodily to Jerusalem. He found himself at the pinnacle of the temple and heard a voice within him say, "If you are God's Anointed, go ahead and jump. Surely God's angels will catch you and carry you to safety, so that you do not so much as strike your foot against a stone; for so it has been written." Resisting this temptation, he said, "I will not put the power of God to such a meaningless test." Suddenly, it seemed he was on a high mountain. There before him he could see the world and all its splendor. He experienced a third temptation. "All this I will give you, all authority and power, if you will place this above all else." Silencing the temptation, Jesus replied, "I choose to worship God alone, and serve only the Holy One." The temptations passed and Jesus felt as if angels were ministering to him.

MISSION AND MINISTRY

✧

Ministry of Jesus

Filled with the power of the Spirit, Jesus began to teach in the synagogues of Galilee. Everywhere he spoke, people praised him.

One sabbath day in Nazareth, he went to the synagogue as was his custom. It was his turn to read the scriptures. The scroll of the prophet Isaiah was handed to him, and he unrolled it to where it was written,

> "The Spirit of God is upon me:
> God has anointed me
> to bring good news to the poor,
> to proclaim release to the captives
> and recovery of sight to the blind,
> to let the oppressed go free,
> and to proclaim the year of God's favor."

After proclaiming the word, he rolled up the scroll, gave it back to the attendant, and sat down. All eyes were fixed upon him. He said, "Today this scripture has been fulfilled in your hearing." Then he expounded on the text. When he was finished speaking, all who were present praised him, amazed at the words that had come from his mouth. "Is this not Mary's son?" the women marveled. And word of him began to spread through the Galilean countryside.

Jesus was about thirty years old when his public ministry began.

First Disciples

One day, as Jesus walked along the Sea of Galilee, he saw Peter and his brother Andrew casting a net into the water, for they were fishermen. Jesus said to them, "Follow me," and they left their nets and followed him. Next he saw James and John, Salome's sons, mending nets in their boat with their father, Zebedee. He called them, and they left their father with the hired men, and followed him.

Jesus called Mary Magdalene. She too followed him, energized by a feeling of freedom and purpose she had never known before. He also called Salome who had supported her sons' decision, and she left the security of her village life to follow after him. Another woman named Mary, respected for her common sense, shocked her neighbors and her sons, James and Joseph, when she said she felt called by Jesus and left to follow him. Susanna decided the moment she met him to become one of his disciples.

Jesus was walking along the water's edge when he saw Matthew sitting at the tax booth. He said to him, "Follow me," and he got up and followed him. Matthew invited Jesus to dinner where he sat and ate with tax collectors and others who were drawn to him, including those who had become his disciples. Later, when it was brought to his attention that some scribes of the Pharisees had criticized him for associating with tax collectors and sinners, Jesus replied, "It is those who are sick, not those who are well, who have need of a physician."

Along the Sea of Galilee Jesus also found Philip, and he said to him, "Follow me." He did. Philip went and told Nathanael that he had found the one long awaited, and that he was Jesus of Nazareth. "Can anything good come out of Nazareth?" Nathanael jeered. Philip said to him, "Come and see." He went, and he too followed Jesus.

Others joined their company: Mary and her husband Cleopas, and Thomas, and James, and Thaddeus, and Simon, and Judas Iscariot. Joanna left her husband, Chuza, and her comfortable life in the palace as the wife of Herod's steward to become a disciple of Jesus. She and other women of wealth used their own personal resources to support Jesus and his mission.

Jesus proclaimed the good news in many cities and villages, accompanied by women and men.

HEALING MIRACLES

✧

Healing Mission

A crowd of Galileans began to follow Jesus and his disciples, for he had healed many people; and all who had diseases tried to get close enough to touch him. Word spread, and people came from Jerusalem and all Judea, even from beyond the Jordan, and from the region around Tyre and Sidon. They brought to him those who were afflicted with various illnesses, and those possessed by evil spirits, and he healed them all.

Peter's Mother-in-Law

After leaving the synagogue in Capernaum where he was teaching on the sabbath, Jesus went to Peter's house. Peter's mother-in-law was sick in bed with a fever. Jesus touched her hand, and the fever left her. From then on, she served him, joining the circle of women who were his followers.

Woman with a Crippling Condition

Jesus was teaching in one of the synagogues on the sabbath when he saw a woman who, for eighteen years, had been severely limited by a crippling condition. She was bent over, unable to straighten up. Jesus called her to him and said to her, "Woman, you are free from your affliction." Then he laid his hands on her. Immediately, she stood up straight, praising God. The leader of the synagogue was appalled that Jesus had dared to heal on the sabbath. He tried to stir up the people, repeating, "There are six days on which work ought to be done. Come then to be healed, not on the sabbath." Jesus said to the bewildered crowd, "Do you not, each one of you, untie your ox or your donkey on the sabbath and lead it from the manger to water? If so, ought not this woman, this daughter of Sarah who has been held in bondage for eighteen long years, be set free on the sabbath?" He had made his point with the people. His opponents lost face as the crowd rejoiced at the wonderful thing he had done.

Woman Who Was Bleeding

As Jesus was walking, the crowds pushed up against him and followed after him. There was a woman among them whose menstrual flow had caused her to bleed continuously for over twelve years. She had spent all she had on physicians, but not a single one could cure her, and she seemed to be getting worse. She had heard about Jesus and had said to herself, "If I could just touch his clothing, I would be well again." She made her way through the crowd and, coming up to him from behind, she courageously touched his garment. Suddenly, she felt her whole body healed of its hemorrhage. Jesus asked, "Who touched me?" When no one responded, Peter said, "People are all around you, pressing in on you. What do you mean, who touched you?" But Jesus insisted, "I felt power flow forth from me. I want to know who touched me." With that, the woman came forward, barely able to contain her joy as she stood there before him. Jesus said to her, "My daughter, your faith was the source of your healing. Be free now, and go in peace."

Servant Who Was Paralyzed

A woman whose husband was a centurion had a servant at home who was severely ill. When Jesus entered Capernaum, she and her husband appealed to him, saying, "Our servant is paralyzed and in terrible distress." Jesus said, "I will come with you and heal your servant," but the woman's husband protested, saying, "Sir, I am not worthy to have you under my roof. Just say the word, and our servant will be healed. I too am a man of authority, with soldiers under my command. I say to one, 'Go,' and he goes, and to another, 'Come,' and he comes; and to my slave, 'Do this,' and he does it." When Jesus heard these words, he said, "The power to heal comes from within, not from authority over another. Let it be done for you as your faith has anticipated." At that moment, their servant was healed.

Sick Child

Jesus returned to Cana in Galilee where he had changed water into wine. There was a woman in Capernaum whose child was critically ill. When she heard that Jesus had returned from Judea to Galilee, she sent her husband, a royal official, to beg Jesus to come and heal their child who was at the point of death, for she knew that he could do it. The official pleaded with Jesus, "Come with me before my little one dies." Jesus said, "Go home. Your child will live." He believed the word that Jesus spoke and began the journey home. Now his wife had sent a messenger to meet him, and long before he reached Capernaum, he heard the good news that his child was alive. He asked the exact time of the child's recovery and was told that the fever had broken the day before at one in the afternoon. This was the moment when Jesus had said to him, "Your child will live." The child's mother had believed in Jesus; now he too became a believer, and with him, their entire household.

Ten with Leprosy

On the way to Jerusalem, Jesus passed through the region between Samaria and Galilee. As he was entering one of the villages there, ten who had been cast out because of a leprous condition called out to him. Keeping their distance, they pleaded with him, saying, "Jesus, master, have mercy on us!" And they were cured of their leprosy. Nine of the ten hurried off to show themselves to the priests so that they might be religiously and socially reinstated. One of them, a woman, when she saw that she was cured, praised God with a loud voice, then threw herself at the feet of Jesus, and thanked him. Jesus asked her, "Were not ten of you healed? Where are the other nine? Are you, a woman, the only one to return and give praise to God?" Then Jesus lifted her up and said, "Go in peace. The strength of your faith has healed you."

Beggar Who Was Blind

Bartimaeus, a beggar who was blind, was sitting by the side of the road as Jesus and his disciples were leaving Jericho. A large crowd accompanied them. When Bartimaeus asked what was causing so much noise and excitement, his sister told him that Jesus of Nazareth was passing by. Hearing that, he shouted at the top of his voice, "Jesus, have mercy on me." Those who were standing near him told him to be quiet. He continued to shout, over and over, "Jesus, have mercy on me." Jesus stopped and said, "Bring him here." His sister helped him to his feet, saying, "Hurry, get up, he is calling you. Trust him with all your heart." He threw off his cloak and stood before Jesus, who asked, "What do you want me to do for you?" He answered, "I want to see." Jesus said, "You will see more than the eye can see. The strength of your faith will heal you." Suddenly, he saw the light and followed Jesus, praising God.

Man Who Was Born Blind

As Jesus was taking his sabbath walk, he saw a man who had been blind from birth. His disciples asked him, "Who has sinned, this man or his parents?" Jesus responded, "Neither this man nor his parents." Then he made some mud from a handful of dirt mixed with his saliva and spread the mud on the man's eyes, saying, "Go and wash in the pool of Siloam." He went and washed and was able to see. His neighbors and those who knew him asked, "Are you not the man who sits and begs? How is it you are able to see?" He replied, "The man called Jesus spread mud on my eyes and told me to wash in Siloam. I washed, and now I see." They brought him to the Pharisees, who also asked him how he had received his sight, and he repeated his story. Referring to Jesus, some of them said, "That man is a sinner; he is not from God, for he does not observe the sabbath." Others, however, disagreed, saying, "How can a sinner perform such signs?" So they said to the man who had once been blind, "What do you say about him? It was your eyes that he opened." He answered, "He is a prophet." Some still doubted, suggesting perhaps that he had never been blind, so they sent for his parents and questioned them. "Is this your son? Was he really born blind? If so, then how does he see?" His mother answered, "This is our son and he was born blind. We do not know how it is that he sees." His father added, "Nor do we know who opened his eyes. He is of age. Ask him. He is able to speak for himself." So they questioned the man a second time, saying, "Glorify God and admit that the man who did this was a sinner." He replied, "I do not know if he is a sinner. I do know I was blind, and now I see." They continued, "What did he do to you? How did he open your eyes?" Exasperated, he said, "I have told you all this already. Why do you ask me again?" Then a heated debate broke out among them, and they concluded by banishing him. When Jesus heard that he had been banished, he sought him out and said to him, "Do you believe in God's Anointed?" He answered, "Who is he, sir? Tell me, so I may believe in him." Jesus said, "You are looking at him." Then he said to Jesus, "I believe."

Man Who Could Not Walk

A woman whose husband could not walk heard that Jesus was teaching nearby in the courtyard of the home of a friend. She summoned her sons and told them to take their father to Jesus. They picked up his bed and followed their mother. They wanted to place him in front of Jesus, but he was in the midst of a very large crowd and they could not get anywhere near him. Knowing that the house had a rooftop patio accessible from outside, the woman sent her sons up to the roof where they lowered the bed over the edge until it lay in front of Jesus. Seeing their determination and moved by their faith, Jesus turned to the man who could not walk and said, "My friend, your sins are forgiven." Among the people gathered were some Pharisees and some teachers of the law. When they heard these words, they were outraged. "You are speaking blasphemy. Who are you to forgive sins? That belongs to God alone." Jesus said, "Which is easier to do: to say, 'Your sins are forgiven,' or 'Get up and walk'?" Then Jesus said to the man lying before him, "Stand up, pick up your bed, and go home." He stood up, rolled up his mat, and walked home, as he and his whole family sang God's praises. All who had seen this were filled with awe at the strange thing they had witnessed.

Boy with Seizures

A couple whose son was severely epileptic brought him to Jesus to be healed, but Jesus was up on the mountain. They begged his disciples to heal him, but they were unable to do so. When Jesus came down from the mountain, a large crowd met him, and the mother of the boy approached him, crying, "Teacher, I beg you, heal my son, for he is my only child. He shrieks and convulses and foams at the mouth and has been like this since he was a baby." The father said, "He falls into the fire and into water. The seizures will surely destroy him. We beg you, have compassion for our child. If you are able, please, help us." Jesus said to the father, "You say to me, 'If you are able.' All things can be done for the one who believes." Pointing to the mother of the boy, the man said, "Sir, she believes. Forgive my unbelief." The boy had a sudden seizure. Jesus held his hand until the seizure had passed and then gave him to his mother. The boy and his parents were transformed by the healing presence of Jesus, and praised the greatness of God.

Canaanite Woman and Her Daughter

Jesus was passing through the territory of Tyre with some of his male disciples. A local woman recognized him. She came up to him and pleaded with him. "Have mercy on me and help me. My daughter is tormented by a troubling spirit." Annoyed, the disciples said, "Get rid of her. She is not a Jew. Tell her to stop bothering us." And they grumbled among themselves. Jesus said to the woman, "They are saying it is unfair to take food from the children and throw it to the dogs." She said, "Tell them the household dogs eat the crumbs that fall from their master's table." Then Jesus said, "Woman, great is your faith. You will have what your heart desires." And the woman's daughter was healed.

Sick and Suffering

Jesus crossed the Sea of Galilee by boat and landed at Gennesaret. As soon as people recognized him, they brought their sick on mats to wherever he happened to be. The sick sought an opportunity just to touch his garment; and all who touched it were healed.

OTHER MIRACLES

✦

Feeding the Multitude

Now Jesus withdrew to a secluded place with some of his disciples in order to rest awhile, for their ministry had been intense. Whole families, however, followed him there, and he felt compassion for them, for they seemed like sheep without a shepherd. He began to teach, and the people kept coming until the crowd was large in number. As it grew late, Jesus said to his disciples, "What shall we give them to eat?" Philip replied, "Six months' wages would not buy enough bread for each one to have just a little." Others said, "Send them away. Let them go into the neighboring villages for food and lodging, for this is an isolated place." But Jesus replied, "Let them eat here. How much food do we have?" Joanna responded, "This boy has five loaves and two fish." Andrew added in disbelief, "What is that among so many?" Jesus said, "Bring it here to me." Then he instructed his disciples to invite the people to sit down together in small groups and prepare to share a meal. Then he blessed the five loaves and the two fish, and he distributed them, and the people began to eat. All ate and all were satisfied. When they were finished, they gathered up the fragments, and they filled twelve baskets with all the food that was left.

Calming the Storm

Jesus was in a boat with his disciples, crossing to the other side of the lake, when a strong wind blew up without warning, whipping the waves with such a force that the boat was in danger of capsizing. Jesus was asleep. Terrified, his disciples woke him, shouting, "Master, we are perishing." Jesus said, "Why are you afraid? Have you no faith?" Then he stood up and spoke to the wind and the sea, and a sudden calm came upon them. His amazed disciples wondered aloud, "What sort of a man is this, that even the winds and the waters obey him?"

Walking on Water

As evening approached, the disciples got into a boat to cross the lake, and Jesus remained behind. He wanted to be by himself, to pray alone there on the mountain. When it grew dark, the disciples were still far from land, for the wind was against them. Then out of the darkness they saw Jesus coming toward them, walking on the water. They were terrified, saying, "It is a ghost." Jesus tried to reassure them, saying, "It is I. Do not be afraid." He got into the boat and the strong wind ceased, and they were utterly astounded.

Life to a Widow's Son

As Jesus was approaching the town of Nain with his disciples and many other people, he saw a large procession of mourners passing through the gate of the town. They were with a widow who was on her way to bury her only son. When Jesus saw her, he felt a deep compassion for her, and said to her, "Do not weep." He touched the bier, and the bearers stood still. Then he said,

"Young man, arise!" The dead son sat up and spoke, and Jesus gave him to his mother. Fear filled all who were standing by. They glorified God, saying, "A great prophet has risen among us," and "God has visited our people." Word spread throughout Judea and the surrounding countryside.

Life to a Little Daughter

The wife of a synagogue official named Jairus had a twelve-year-old daughter who was dying. She sent her husband to plead with Jesus to come and save their child. He threw himself at the feet of Jesus and begged him to come with him. "Come and lay your hands on her, that she may recover and live." Jesus went with him, and as they were walking, a messenger ran up to Jairus with this tragic word from his wife: "Our little girl is dead. Do not trouble the teacher any further." Jesus said, "Do not despair. Your child will live. Continue to believe." When he came to the house and heard the weeping and wailing of the mourners, he said, "Do not weep, she is only sleeping," but they knew that she was dead. The mother brought him to her daughter's room. He took the child by the hand and said to her, "Little girl, get up." She got up and ran to her mother, and asked her for something to eat, and everyone was astounded at this thing that had occurred.

WOMEN IN THE LIFE OF JESUS

✧

Mary Magdalene

Mary Magdalene, a strong and spirited woman, was a leader among the Galilean women who were disciples of Jesus. Some of the men found it difficult to share status with a woman. Others envied her privileged position. Peter and his brother Andrew complained that Jesus seemed to favor her, for he would tell her things he did not share with them. One of the women once said to Peter, "Why are you so hostile to her? She is not an adversary. If Jesus finds her worthy, who are you to reject her?" The female disciples respected Mary for her competence and her wisdom. A circle formed around her of women who ministered to other women with compassion and empathy.

Martha and Mary

Jesus loved Martha and her sister Mary. They lived in the village of Bethany, just outside of Jerusalem. He was often with them, sharing a meal, confiding in them, telling them of his ministry and mission. Martha was outgoing and vocal, while Mary was reticent and subdued. Mary would often listen quietly while her sister engaged Jesus in a lively exchange.

One day their brother Lazarus fell critically ill. They sent a message to Jesus, saying, "The one whom you love is dying." Although Lazarus was his friend, Jesus delayed two days before saying to his disciples, "We are returning to Judea." They said to him, "Rabbi, they tried to stone you there. Why are you going back?" He answered, "Because Lazarus has fallen asleep, and I am going there to awaken him." The disciples said to Jesus, "If he has fallen asleep, he will be all right," for they all knew of his illness. Then Jesus told them plainly, "Lazarus is dead. Let us go to his sisters."

On hearing that Jesus was approaching Bethany, Martha went out to meet him. Mary stayed at home, for the house was filled with mourners who had come to console the women on the death of their brother. When Martha saw Jesus, she said to him, "Friend, if you had only been here, my brother would not have died. Yet I know, even now, that God will grant you anything you ask." Jesus said to her, "Your brother will rise again." Martha replied, "I know that he will rise again at the final resurrection." Jesus said to her, "I am the resurrection and the life. Those who believe in me will live, even though they die, and whoever lives believing in me, will never die. Do you believe this?" Martha said to Jesus, "Yes, I believe that you are God's Anointed whom God has sent into the world."

Martha ran to call her sister. "Mary, he is here, and he is asking for you." Mary went out to meet him. Those who were with her, consoling her, hurried after her, for they thought she was going to the tomb to weep. Mary fell at the feet of Jesus, crying, "If you had been here, he would not have died." When he saw her tears, and the tears of those supporting her, he was overcome with compassion, and he too began to weep. Some of the mourners whispered, "See how much he loved him," while others murmured among themselves, "He opened the eyes of the man born blind; could he not have prevented the death of his friend?" Jesus asked, "Where have you laid him?" and Mary answered, "Come and see."

Grieving, Jesus came to the tomb, a cave with a stone before it. "Roll away the stone," he said, in a voice charged with emotion. Martha interrupted. "He has been dead four days now; the stench will be appalling." But Jesus insisted, saying, "Have I not told you that if you believe, you will see the glory of God?" They removed the stone and Jesus shouted, "Lazarus come out!" The dead man came out, his limbs bound with burial bands, his face wrapped in a cloth. Jesus said to those who were standing near, "Unbind him and set him free." Many who had come to Bethany to mourn and had witnessed the raising of Lazarus now believed in Jesus, but some went to report him to the chief priests and Pharisees.

Martha and Mary prepared a big dinner to honor the return of Lazarus, and Jesus and many of his disciples joined in the celebration. Mary took some of her costly perfume and poured it over the feet of Jesus. Its fragrance filled the room. Then she wiped his feet with her hair. Judas Iscariot complained bitterly. "Why was this perfume not sold and the money given to the poor?" Judas cared nothing at all for the poor. As keeper of their common purse, and secretly a thief, he could have had access to Mary's money because she was one of them, and he resented such waste. Jesus said, "Do not be annoyed with her for so lavishly anointing me. The poor will always be with you. You will not always have me."

After the meal, Mary sat listening to Jesus, content just to be with him. Seeing that her sister seemed to be preoccupied with far too much to do, Lazarus said to Mary, "Why let her do all the work by herself?" Jesus interrupted him, "Your sister has chosen to be present to me and that is the best part of my being with you. Do not take that away from me."

Samaritan Woman

Jesus left Judea and was passing through Samaria on his return to Galilee when he came to the city of Sychar, the site of Jacob's well. It was midday, and he was tired. His disciples went into the city to buy something to eat, and they left him sitting by the well.

A woman came to draw water. Jesus said to her, "May I have a drink?" She said to him, "How can you, a Jew, ask me, a woman of Samaria, for a drink?" For Jews and Samaritans were estranged. Jesus said to her, "By asking you, I am offering you a sip of living water." The woman replied, "You have no bucket and the well is deep. How will you get this life-giving water? Are you greater than our ancestor Jacob who gave our village this well?" Jesus said to her, "Whoever drinks of this water will continue to be thirsty, but those who drink of the water I give will never thirst again. The water I give will become in them a wellspring of eternal life." The woman said to Jesus, "Sir, give me this water, so I never have to draw from this well again, so I never thirst again." Jesus said to the woman, "Go and call those in the community with whom you share a relationship with God and bring them back with you." "I have no relationship with God," the woman replied. "Indeed, you have no relationship with God," he said, "for you have been searching for God through a variety of religious experiences, and now you are affiliated with a tradition to which you are not committed." "So you are a prophet," the woman said. "Then explain this point to me. Our ancestors worshiped here on this mountain, yet Jews say that Jerusalem is the place where people must worship." Jesus said, "Woman, the time is coming when you will worship God neither on this mountain nor in Jerusalem, but in spirit and in truth. God is spirit. The time will come — it is already here — when true worshipers will worship God in spirit and in truth." She said, "I know the Messiah is coming, and he will speak truth to us when he comes." Jesus said, "I am he."

The disciples returned and they were amazed that he was speaking with a Samaritan woman, but none of them dared to say to him, "Why are you talking to her?" The woman left her water jar and hurried into the city, saying, "Come and see a man who has told me everything I have ever done. Can this man be the Messiah?" Many left the city and followed her to Jesus.

Meanwhile, the disciples were urging Jesus, "Rabbi, have something to eat." But he replied, "I have food to eat which you do not know about." They looked at one another. "Who do you suppose could have given him food?" Jesus said, "My food is to do the will of the One who sent me, and to accomplish God's work."

Many Samaritans believed in Jesus on the strength of the woman's testimony, that he had revealed what she had not told. He remained in Sychar for two full days. After that many more believed in him, saying, "We have heard for ourselves, and we too believe he is the savior of the world."

A Woman Accused

At daybreak, Jesus returned to the temple, and people crowded around him as he began to teach. The scribes and Pharisees dragged a woman into his presence, and in full view of everyone, made this accusation. "Rabbi," they said, "this woman here has been caught in the act of adultery. The Law commands us to stone her to death. Tell us, what do you say?" Now this was a test, for they were looking for something to use against him. Jesus bent down, and with the tip of his finger, started scribbling on the ground. They kept repeating their question. Jesus stood up and said to them, "Let the one among you who has not sinned be the first to throw a stone." Then bending down, he scribbled some more as, one by one, those who had condemned her silently slipped away. When Jesus was alone with the woman, he said, "Where have your accusers gone? Has no one here condemned you?" "No one, sir," she responded. "Neither do I condemn you," said Jesus. "Go now and sin no more."

A Woman Anoints Jesus

Simon, a Pharisee, invited Jesus to a meal at his house. When Jesus was seated at the table, a local woman with a bad reputation came into the room carrying an alabaster jar of ointment. She stood behind Jesus, weeping, then bent down to anoint his feet. Her tears fell on the feet of Jesus, and she wiped them away with her hair. She kissed his feet and anointed them with the ointment from her jar. Seeing this, Simon said to himself, "If this man were really a prophet, he would know what kind of woman this is; he would know her reputation; he would know who was touching him." Jesus said to him, "Simon, I have something to say to you. A creditor had two debtors. The one owed him five hundred denarii, the other owed him fifty. Since neither was able to pay him back, he canceled the debts for both of them. Which one loved him more?" Simon replied, "I suppose the one with the greater debt." And Jesus replied, "Indeed." Then Jesus said, "Simon, I came into your house, and you, the host, brought no water for my feet, but this woman washed my feet with her tears and dried them with her hair. You gave me no kiss in greeting me, but she has been covering my feet with kisses from the moment I arrived. You did not anoint my head with oil, but she has anointed my feet with ointment. You say her sins are many. Well, I say her sins are forgiven her because she has loved so much. And she has forgiven you your sin, because of her great love." Then he said to the woman, "Your sins are forgiven." Those at table were outraged. "Who is he to forgive sins?" they said among themselves. "And what could possibly be the sin that he said she has forgiven us?" Then Jesus turned to the woman and said, "Your faith has been your salvation. Go now in peace." The woman left, and soon after that joined the company of female disciples.

PARABLES

✦

Jesus spoke in parables to teach people how to discern the hidden ways of God, for many look but seldom see, listen but fail to hear, perceive but do not understand.

Delinquent Daughter and Her Sister

A woman had two daughters. The elder remained with her mother. The younger, more independent, took what had been her dowry and ran away from home. When her money was gone, she supported herself through begging and prostitution. One day, penniless and pregnant and filled with remorse at her meaningless life, she made up her mind, despite her shame, to return home to her mother. She imagined what she would say to her. "Let me live here as a servant until I earn the right to be called your child."

She set out on her journey home. When she was still a long way off, her mother saw her coming and ran all the way to meet her. She threw her arms around her child, kissed her, and held her close. Her daughter said, "Mother, I have acted foolishly. I have sinned against you and God. I do not deserve to be called your child." But her mother dressed her in a brand new robe, gave her bracelets and earrings and rings, and sandals for her feet. She killed a fatted calf and prepared a feast to celebrate her return. "My baby lives, the one who was dead. My lost child has been found," she sang, and they feasted into the night.

Now the girl's older sister was silent and aloof as the celebrating went on. She refused to join in the dancing. She was angered by the songs. Her mother came and pleaded with her not to be resentful, but she was bitter in her reply. "All these years, I have stayed at home and worked like a slave for you. I have never been disobedient, nor have I ever complained, yet when have you thrown a feast for me, or prepared a special meal that I might celebrate with my friends? But when this delinquent daughter of yours gets pregnant and comes back home, you kill the fatted calf for her." Then the mother said to her firstborn child, "My daughter, you have always been with me, and all that is mine is yours. I am sorry I have neglected you. Forgive your sister and me. Then let us rejoice that you and your sister are fully alive once more, that you who felt lost and your sister who was lost have both been found again."

Good Samaritan

A woman somewhere between Jerusalem and Jericho fell into the hands of unscrupulous men who raped her and abused her, and left her lying by the side of the road, badly beaten and barely conscious. Now by chance a priest was going down that road. When he saw her, he was filled with disgust, and passed by on the other side. A very important person mistook her to be a prostitute, and for a moment he was tempted, then passed by on the other side. A foreigner, a Samaritan, saw her and was filled with compassion for her. He went over to her, washed her wounds, and tried to comfort her. Then he lifted her onto his donkey and brought her to an inn. The innkeeper tried to avoid taking her — he had seen her kind before — but the innkeeper's wife found a room for her and put her to bed for the night. The next morning, the Samaritan took out some money and gave it to the innkeeper's wife, saying, "Please take care of her. And when I return, I will repay whatever else you spend."

Now which of these was neighbor to the woman violated by unscrupulous men?

Foolish Woman

The gardens of a wealthy woman produced abundantly. She said to herself, "What shall I do, for I have no place to store my food?" Then she said, "I will demolish my pantries and my root cellars, and I will build bigger ones, and there I will store my vegetables and fruits, my seeds and herbs and grains. And I will say to my soul, 'Relax! Eat, drink, be merry; you have food enough for years.'" But God said, "Foolish woman! Your life will end this very night. And all those things you have kept for yourself, whose now will they be?"

So it is with those who hoard their wealth and are impoverished in the eyes of God.

Do Not Worry

Do not worry about your life, what you will eat, or what you will drink, or about your body, what you will wear. Life is more than food and the body is more than clothing. Look at the birds of the air. They neither sift the flour nor shape the loaves, yet they eat because God feeds them. Are you not as valuable as they? Can you by worrying add a single hour to your short span of life?

And why do you worry about clothing? Consider the lilies of the field. See how they grow; they neither toil nor spin, yet Bathsheba in all her glory was never clothed like one of these. But if God so clothes the grass of the field, which is here today and tomorrow is gone, God will surely clothe you. Therefore, do not worry, saying, "What will we eat?" or "What will we drink?" or "What are we going to wear?" God knows you need all these things. Strive to be one with the will of God and you will be given all that you need.

Widow and Judge

There was a judge who had no fear of God and no respect for people. There was a widow who kept coming to him, saying, "Grant me justice," for someone was oppressing her. The judge refused to listen. But after awhile he said to himself, "This widow will wear me out by continually coming with her complaint. I will grant her the justice she desires, so she stops bothering me."

Even so God will grant justice to those who cry to Her day and night. Will She delay in helping them? I tell you, She will act quickly, granting justice to them.

Noblewoman and Serving Maid

Two women went up to the temple to pray. One was a noblewoman and the other was a serving maid. The noblewoman stood erect and prayed, "I thank you, God, that I am not like others: prostitutes, gossips, liars, thieves, or like my serving maid. I fast twice a week; I am generous with all I own." But the serving maid bowed her head and prayed, "Oh God, be merciful to me, a sinner." The serving maid found favor with God; not so, the noblewoman.

Lost Coin

What woman, having lost a silver coin, does not light a lamp, sweep the house, and search until she finds it? When she has found it, she calls her neighbors and friends, saying, "Come, now, and rejoice with me, for I found the coin I had lost." Just so, I tell you, there is joy in heaven over one sinner who repents.

Lost Sheep

Which one of you, having a hundred sheep and losing one of them, does not leave the ninety-nine in the wilderness to look for the one that is lost? When it is found, she whispers a word of thanks and leads it home, rejoicing. Then she calls her friends and neighbors and says, "Come, now, and rejoice with me, for I found my sheep that was lost." Just so, I tell you, there will be more joy in heaven over one sinner who repents than over ninety-nine who need no repentance.

Yeast

To what shall I compare the household of God? It is like a woman who put a little yeast into a lot of flour and made many large loaves with it. It is like the yeast that the woman kneaded into the flour until all of it was leavened.

Mustard Seed

What is the household of God like? It is like a mustard seed, the smallest of seeds, planted in a garden where it grew into a tree, a very large tree, so that the birds of the air made nests in its branches.

Barren Fig Tree

A woman had a fig tree which she had planted in her courtyard. When she came to pick fruit, she found none. So she said to her gardener, "For three years I have come to pick fruit from this fig tree, and this year again it has none. Enough! Cut it down! Why should it suck nutrients from the soil?" The gardener said, "Let it live another year. I will dig around it and fertilize it. If it does not bear fruit next year, then we can cut it down."

Laborers in the Vineyard

The household of heaven is like a woman hiring laborers for her vineyard. Early in the morning, her steward brought some laborers to her, and when they had agreed on a daily wage, she sent them into her vineyard. The steward went out around nine o'clock and saw others standing in the marketplace. He said to them, "Go and work in the vineyard, and you will be paid whatever is right." So they went. At noon and again around three o'clock, he went out and did the same. At five o'clock the steward went out and found some others and asked, "Why are you standing here idle?" and they said, "Because no one has hired us." He said to them, "Go into the vineyard." When evening came, the owner of the vineyard arranged payment of their wages. She said to the steward, "Pay the laborers this amount, from the last hired to the first." Those hired around five o'clock received the full daily wage. Those hired first expected more, but they received the same amount. They complained to the owner, saying, "These last worked only one hour and you have made them equal to us, yet we have withstood the heat and have borne the burden of the day." She replied, "Friends, I do you no wrong. Did you not agree on the usual daily wage? Take what is yours and go. So what if I choose to give to these last the same as I give to you. Am I not allowed to do what I choose with what belongs to me? Or are you jealous because I am generous?"

Even so the last will be first, and the first will be last. Such is the household of heaven.

MORE PARABLES

✧

Parable of the Rich and the Poor

There was a wealthy woman who wore purple and fine fabric and who feasted sumptuously every day. At her gate lay a poor woman, covered with sores, who longed to satisfy her hunger with what fell from the rich woman's table. The dogs that ate what fell from the table would come and lick the poor woman's sores.

The poor woman died and was carried away by angels to be with Sarah. The rich woman died and was doomed to endure the fierce, fiery torment of her insensitivity. Looking up, she saw Sarah far off in the distance, with the poor woman at her side. She called out, "Mother Sarah, have pity on me. Send that woman to help me. Let her dip the tip of her finger in water and bestow on me a blessing, for I am in agony." But Sarah said, "Child, you received good things during your lifetime and she endured evil things; now you are the one who suffers, while she is comforted here. There is a great chasm between you and us, so that no one can cross from there to here, or from here to there, no matter how much we might want to." She said, "Then I beg you, send her to my mother's house to warn my five sisters, so that they may change their ways." Sarah replied, "They have Miriam and other prophets. Let them listen to them." She said,

"No, mother Sarah, they will not listen; but if someone visits them from the dead, they will repent." Sarah said, "If they do not listen to Miriam and the other prophets, neither will they be convinced if someone rises from the dead."

Two Daughters

A woman had two daughters. She went to the first and said, "Child, work with the women today." She answered, "I will not," but later changed her mind and went. The mother went to the second daughter and said the same to her. She said to her mother, "I will," but then she did not go. Which of the two did the will of her mother?

Dishonest Administrator

There was a wealthy woman who had hired another woman as administrator of her estate. One day it was reported to her that this woman was stealing her property. So she summoned her and said to her, "What is this I hear about you? Hand over your accounts to me, for you can hold the position no longer." The administrator said to herself, "What will I do? For she is taking away my livelihood. I do not want to work with my hands, and I will not beg for my living." Then suddenly she said, "I know what to do, so that when I am dismissed as administrator, people will welcome me into their homes." She summoned her employer's debtors and spoke to them, one by one. She asked the first, "How much do you owe my employer?" She answered, "A hundred jugs of olive oil." She said to her, "Make it fifty." She asked another, "How much do you owe?" She replied, "A hundred containers of wheat." She said, "Make it eighty." The wealthy woman commended her dishonest administrator because she had acted shrewdly. The people of this world show far more ingenuity in handling their affairs than do those who are committed to the world to come.

Unforgiving Employee

Heaven may be compared to a woman who decided to settle accounts with those employed by her. One owed her an enormous sum. Since she was unable to repay the debt, her employer ordered her possessions to be sold so that payment might be made. The employee fell to her knees, pleading, "Have patience with me, and I will repay you everything I owe." Out of pity for her, the employer reconsidered and forgave her the entire debt. As the employee went out, she met one of her peers who owed her a paltry sum. Seizing her, she said, "Pay what you owe." Her colleague begged her, "Have patience with me, and I will repay you everything I owe." She refused and sent the woman to prison until she could pay her debt. The others were greatly distressed at this, and they reported it to their employer. The woman summoned her employee and said, "You wicked woman! I forgave you your entire debt because you pleaded with me. Should you not have had mercy on your peer, as I had mercy on you?" Then she handed her over to the authorities until she repaid her entire debt. So will it be done to us if we do not forgive our sister or our brother from our heart.

Wicked Tenants

A woman leased her vineyard to tenants before she left the country. At harvest time, she sent someone to collect from the tenants her share of the vineyard's yield, but they seized her representative, beat her, and sent her away empty-handed. The owner sent others with the same request, but they mistreated them as well. Finally, she sent her daughter, saying, "Surely, they will respect my child." But when the tenants saw her, they said, "She is the heir. Let us kill her and seize her inheritance." And they did. Now when the owner of the vineyard comes, what will she do to those tenants?

Assessing One's Resources

Which one of you, intending to build, does not first sit down and estimate the cost, to see whether you have enough to complete the structure? Otherwise, when you have laid the foundation and then find you are unable to finish, all who see it will ridicule you, saying, "This woman began to build, and she was not able to finish."

Or what leader, about to confront an opposing force, will not first sit down and consider whether she is able, with this many resources, to take on an opponent who has twice that amount. If not, then sometime before the confrontation, she sends a delegation to negotiate peace.

The Banquet

A woman prepared a banquet and invited many guests. When it was time to begin the festivities, she sent her servant to say to those invited, "Come, now, for everything is ready." But all of them made excuses. The first said to her, "My daughter has recently given birth and I must remain with her. I am sorry, I cannot come." Another said, "My loaves of bread are rising and I must stay and bake them. I am sorry, I cannot come." Another said,

"I have just been married, so of course, I cannot come." The woman was disappointed with this response and so she said to her servant, "Go into the streets and lanes of the town. Bring back those who are impoverished and those who have been left out." When the maid returned, she said to her, "What you ordered has been done, and still there is room." The woman said, "Go, search the roads and secluded paths. Urge people to come to my banquet, so that my house may be filled. And none of those invited will ever taste what I have prepared."

Ten Bridesmaids

Ten bridesmaids took their lamps and went out to meet the bride. Five were said to be foolish, and five were said to be wise. The five considered foolish took no extra oil with them, but the five who were considered wise took additional flasks of oil. Because the wedding party was delayed, all of them became drowsy, and all ten fell asleep. At midnight, a shout awakened them. "Look! Here come the bride and groom! Let us go and meet them." The bridesmaids arose and trimmed their lamps. Five of them said to the others, "Give us some of your extra oil, for our lamps are going out." But they responded, "No! There may not be enough for you and for us. You had better go to one of the dealers and buy some for yourselves." So the women went to find some oil, and while they were gone, the couple arrived, and those who were present went in with them to share the wedding banquet; and the door was shut behind them. Later, the other bridesmaids came, saying, "Please, open the door for us." Instead, they heard the bridegroom say, "I tell you, I do not know you."

Now which of these bridesmaids were really prepared to enter the household of heaven?

Haves and Have-Nots

A woman going on a journey summoned three of her servants and entrusted her money to them according to her determination of each one's ability. To one she gave a large amount, to another, half as much, and to the third, very little. While she was away, the one to whom she had given the most invested the woman's money, doubling her investment. The second, who had received half as much, went out and did the same. The one who had received but a small amount dug a hole and buried it. After some time, the woman returned to her estate to settle accounts with them. The one to whom she had given the most came forward and handed her twice as much, saying, "You gave me this much money, and I have doubled that amount." The woman praised her, saying, "Well done, good and responsible servant. You have been trustworthy in a few things; I will put you in charge of many. Come and enjoy your reward." The one who had received half as much came forward and handed her twice that amount, saying, "You gave me this much money; look, I have doubled that amount." The woman praised that one as well, saying, "Well done, good and responsible servant. You have been trustworthy in a few things; I will put you in charge of many. Come and enjoy your reward." Then the one who had received a small amount also came forward, saying, "I knew you were a harsh woman, reaping where you had not sown, gathering crops where you had not planted. I was afraid to risk your wrath, so I hid your money and kept it safe. I am returning what is yours."

The woman replied, "You wicked and lazy servant! You knew that I reaped where I had not sown, that I gathered what I had not planted. Then you should have deposited my money in a bank, so that I could have received some interest." Then the woman said, "Take the money from her and give it to the one who has the most. For to all those who have, more will be given, and they will have an abundance; as for those who have nothing, even the little they have will be taken away from them."

Now which of these really belongs among those in the household of heaven?

The Treasure

Heaven is like a treasure hidden in a field, which someone finds and hides again until, rejoicing, she sells all that she has and is able to buy that field.

The Pearl

Heaven is like someone in search of fine pearls. When she finally finds a pearl of great value, she sells all that she has and buys it.

The Net

Heaven is like a net that is thrown into the sea and catches fish of every kind. When the net is full, it is drawn ashore, and the good are put into baskets while the bad are thrown away.

Seed

To what shall we compare the household of heaven? To someone who scatters seed on the ground, who sleeps nights and rises days, while the seed germinates and grows, she knows not how. The earth produces of itself, first the stalk, then the head, then the full grain of wheat. And when the grain is ripe, she goes in with her sickle, because the harvest has come.

Weeds

The household of heaven may be compared to someone who sowed good seed in her field; then while she was asleep, an enemy came and sowed weeds among the wheat. When the plants came up and bore grain, the weeds came up as well. The servants said to the householder, "Did you not sow good seed in your field? Then where did these weeds come from?" She answered, "An enemy has done this." Her servants said, "Do you want us to go and pull them up?" She replied, "No; if you pull up the weeds, you will pull up the wheat as well. Let both of them grow until the harvest. Then at harvest time, I will tell the reapers to first go and gather the weeds and bind them in bundles for burning before putting the wheat in my barn."

Sower

A sower went out to sow. Seed fell along the path, but the birds came by and ate it. Seed fell on rocky ground, but the sun rose, scorching it, and without roots, it withered away. Seed fell among thorns, but the thorns eventually choked it. Seed fell into good soil and brought forth grain abundantly, yielding a hundredfold.

Parable of the Sower Explained

Let those who have ears, listen! The seed is the word of God. Those on the path are the ones who have heard;

then the evil one snatches the word from their hearts, so they cannot believe and be saved. Those on the rock are the ones who hear the word and receive it with joy. But they have no root; they believe only for a little while, then when they are tested by trouble or persecution, they immediately fall away. Those among thorns hear the word, but the cares of the world, and the lure of wealth, and a desire for the pleasures of life choke the word, and it does not mature within them. Those that are in the good soil hear the word and hold it fast, bearing fruit with patient endurance.

Use of Parables

With many parables such as these, Jesus spoke the word to them, as they were able to hear it; and he explained the parables to his disciples.

TEACHINGS OF JESUS

Whenever Jesus saw the crowds — by the lake, in the village, in the synagogue, or on the road as he was walking from place to place — he spoke with them, and listened to them, and taught them many things.

Love

The first commandment is, love God with all your heart, and with all your soul, and with all your mind, and with all your strength. The second is, love your neighbor as yourself.

Now I give you a new commandment, that you love one another as I have loved you.

Everyone should know that you are my disciples by your love for one another. Yes, this is my commandment: that you love one another as I have loved you. There is no greater love than to lay down one's life for one's friends.

If you love me, you will keep my commandments; and those who love me will be loved by God, and I will love them and reveal myself to them.

As God has loved me, so have I loved you. Abide in my love.

Love Your Enemies

Love your enemies, do good to those who hate you, pray for those who abuse you. And do not withhold even your shawl from the one who takes your coat. If anyone takes away your goods, do not ask for them back again.

If you love those who love you, what credit is that to you? Even sinners love those who love them. If you do good to those who do good to you, what credit is that to you? For even sinners do as much. If you lend to those who will give something in return, what credit is that to you? Even sinners lend to sinners to receive something back. Love your enemies, do good, and lend, expecting nothing in return.

Be merciful as God is merciful, and God, whose children you are, will reward you.

Settle with Your Opponents

Determine for yourselves what is right. Negotiate with your accuser and make an effort to settle your debts on your own, or you may be dragged before a judge who may put you in prison until you have paid every penny of what you owe.

Do Not Judge

Do not judge, so you will not be judged; do not condemn, and you will not be condemned. For you will be judged with the judgement you make.

Can someone who is blind guide another who is blind? Then how can you see the speck in your neighbor's eye and ignore the debris in your own? And how can you say to your neighbor, "Let me remove the speck from your eye," while debris remains in your own? First remove the debris from your own eye, and you will see clearly enough to remove the speck from the eye of your neighbor.

Humility

When you are invited to a dinner, do not sit at the place of honor, in case someone more distinguished than you has been invited by your host; and the host who invited both of you would then have to come and say to you, "Give your place to this person," and in disgrace you would have to move to the lowest place. When you are invited, sit down at the lowest place, so that when your host comes, she may say to you, "Friend, move up higher." Then you will be honored in the presence of all who sit at the table with you. For all who exalt themselves will be humbled; and all who humble themselves will be exalted.

Self-Deception

On that day many will say, "Did we not prophesy in your name, and cast out demons in your name, and do many deeds of power in your name?" But I will say to them, "I never knew you. Depart from me. For not everyone who ministers in my name will enter into heaven, but only those who do the will of God."

Other Ministers

John said to Jesus, "Teacher, we saw someone else driving out demons in your name, and we tried to stop her because she is not one of us." But Jesus said, "Do not stop her. Whoever is not against us is for us."

Prayer

Whatever you ask for in prayer, believe that you have received it, and it will be given to you.

Whenever you pray, forgive, if you have anything against anyone, so that God may also forgive you your sins.

When you pray, do not stand in a public place so that you may be seen by others.

When you pray, go to your room and shut the door, and pray to God in private.

When you are praying, do not multiply empty phrases, assuming you will be heard because of your many words. God knows what you need, even before you ask.

When you pray, pray in words that are similar to these:

> Our Mother, our Father,
> in heaven and on earth,
> holy is Your name.
> May Your justice come,
> Your will be done,
> on earth as it is in heaven.
> Give us this day our daily bread.
> And forgive us our sins,
> as we forgive those who sin against us.
> Do not put us to the test,
> but deliver us from evil.

Perseverance in Prayer

Suppose you have a friend, and you go to her house at midnight and say, "Lend me three loaves of bread, for a friend of mine has come unexpectedly, and I have nothing to give her." And she answers from within, "Do not bother me. The door is locked and my children are asleep. I cannot help you now." I assure you, although she will not get up and help you because you are her friend, if you persist, she will surely get up and give you whatever you need.

Ask, and it will be given to you; seek, and you will find; knock, and the door will be opened to you. For everyone who asks will receive, everyone who seeks will find, and for everyone who knocks, the door will open. Now which one of you would give a stick if your child asks for a fish? Or who would give a stone to the child who asks for an egg? If you then, who are human, give good gifts to your children, how much more will God our Mother give the Spirit of Wisdom to those who pray to Her?

Fasting

They said to Jesus, "John's disciples often fast, but your disciples eat and drink." Jesus said, "Why should the wedding guests fast when the bride and the bridegroom are with them? The day will come when they are taken from them, and that is when they will fast."

When you fast, do not look dismal so as to show others that you are fasting, for that is hypocritical, and you will have received your reward. When you fast, anoint your head and wash your face, so that your fasting may not be seen by others, but only by God, who will reward you.

Presence of Jesus

Where two or more of you are gathered in my name, I am there among you. Remember, I am with you always.

Spirit

God will send you an Advocate to be with you forever. This is the Spirit of truth who abides with you and is in you.

The Spirit, whom God will send in my name, will teach you everything, and remind you of all that I have said to you.

The wind blows where it chooses. You hear its sound but you do not know where it comes from or where it goes. So it is with the Spirit.

Hospitality

When you give a luncheon or dinner, do not invite your rich neighbors or those who will invite you in return, for then you will be similarly repaid. If you invite your relatives or your sisters or your friends, you will surely be repaid. Rather, invite those who are impoverished and those who have been excluded, and you will be blessed for they will enrich you in unexpected ways.

Rewards

Whoever welcomes you welcomes me, and whoever welcomes me welcomes the one who sent me. Whoever welcomes a prophet in the name of a prophet will receive a prophet's reward; and whoever welcomes a holy person in the name of a holy person will receive a holy person's reward; and whoever gives even a cup of cold water to one of these little ones in the name of a disciple will receive their reward.

Almsgiving

Give to anyone who begs from you, and do not refuse anyone who would borrow from you.

Beware of practicing your piety before others in order to be seen by them, for God will not reward you.

Whenever you give alms, do not sound a trumpet as hypocrites do, in order to be praised by others, for you will have received your reward. When you give alms, do not let your left hand know what your right hand is doing. Let your almsgiving be done inconspicuously and God, who sees all, will reward you.

Peace

Be at peace with one another. Peace I leave with you, my peace I give to you. Do not let your hearts be troubled, and do not be afraid.

Learn how to recognize the things that make for peace. Be attentive at every moment to receiving a revelation from God.

Reconciliation

If, when you are offering your gift at the altar, you remember that your sister or your brother has something against you, leave your gift, go and be reconciled, and then come and make your offering.

Hypocrisy

Beware of hypocrisy, for everything that is covered will be uncovered, and everything that is secret will be made known. What you say in the dark will be heard in the light, and what you whisper behind closed doors will be shouted from the rooftops.

Self-Justification

Do not justify yourself in the sight of others, for what is prized by human beings is often an abomination to God, and God knows what is in your heart.

Marriage

The One who made humanity from the beginning "made them female and male," and for this reason, a woman and a man leave mother and father in order to be joined together, so that the two become one flesh. God has joined them together; they are no longer two, but one.

Life

You search the scriptures because you think that in them you have eternal life, that it is they that testify on my behalf. Come to me. Seek life in me. I came that you may have life, and have it in all its fullness.

It is the spirit that gives life. The words that I have spoken to you are spirit and life.

Those who try to hang on to their life will lose it, but those who give up their life will keep it. Unless a grain of wheat falls into the earth and dies, it remains just a single grain; but if it dies, it bears much fruit.

Anyone who hears my word and believes in the One who sent me has passed from death to life and has eternal life.

Be Ready

Be dressed for action and have your lamps lit, like maids waiting for the lady of the house to return, that they may open the door for her when she knocks. Blessed are those maids whom she finds waiting for her, even if she comes in the middle of the night, or just before dawn. She will invite them to sit at table with her and will serve them something to eat.

If a woman knew when a thief was coming, she would protect her home against theft. Be ready, for God's Anointed will come at an unexpected hour.

About that day and hour no one knows, only God knows. Therefore, you must be ready. Stay awake, because you do not know on what day your God is coming.

In the Name of Jesus

I will do whatever you ask in my name, so that God may be glorified in me. If you ask me for anything in my name, I will do it for you. If you ask anything of God in my name, God will give it to you.

Sorrow into Joy

You will weep and mourn, but the world will rejoice; you will have pain, yet your pain will turn into joy. When a woman is in labor, she has pain, because her hour has come. But when her child is born, she forgets the anguish because of the joy she feels in having brought new life into the world. So it is that you have pain now; but I will see you again and your hearts will rejoice, and that joy no one will take from you.

Word of God

In the beginning was the word, and the word was with God, and the word was God. And the word became flesh and lives among us.

Whoever is from God hears the words of God. The

words that I have spoken to you are spirit and life. Those who love me will keep my word, and God will love them, and we will come to them and will make our home with them.

WISDOM OF JESUS

✧

The wisdom sayings of Jesus are many; no single book could hold them.

Beatitudes

Blessed are you who are poor, for you are precious to God.

Blessed are you who are hungry now, for you will be satisfied.

Blessed are you who weep now, for one day you will laugh.

Blessed are you who put others first, for you will inherit the earth.

Blessed are you who show mercy, for mercy will be shown to you.

Blessed are you who are singlehearted, for you will see God.

Blessed are you who make peace, for you will be called the children of God.

Blessed are you when people hate you, and exclude you, and persecute you on account of the word made flesh through you and the wisdom at work within you, for your reward is great in heaven.

Salt

You are the salt of the earth. But if salt has lost its savor, it cannot be restored. It is no longer good for anything, but is simply thrown away. Do not lose your savor, for you are the salt of the earth.

Light

You are the light of the world. A city on a hill cannot be hidden. No one puts a lighted lamp under a bushel basket. They put it high on a lampstand, where it gives light to all in the house. In the same way, let your own light shine, so that others may see the good that you do and give glory to God our Creator.

Seeing

The eye is the lamp of the body. If you see clearly, your whole being will radiate with light. But if your vision is distorted, the light will not be in you.

Giving

Give and it will be given to you: a generous amount, pressed down, shaken together, running over, will be poured into your lap, and still more will be given to you; for what you give will be what you get back.

A Tree and Its Fruit

Each tree is known by its own fruit. A good tree does not bear bad fruit, nor does a bad tree bear good fruit. Figs are not gathered from thorns, nor are grapes picked from thistles. A good person produces good out of the good treasure of the heart. An evil person produces evil from the evil in the heart. From the fullness of the heart, the mouth speaks.

Two Foundations

Who hears my words and acts on them is like someone who, when building a house, dug deep and laid the foundation on rock. When the flood came and the river overflowed, it battered the house but could not shake it, because it had been well built. But the one who hears and does not act is like someone who built a house on sand without a firm foundation. When the river rose, the house fell, and all of it was ruined.

Fear Not

Do not fear those who kill the body, and after that can do nothing more. Fear those who, after they have killed, have authority to cast into hell. Are not five sparrows sold for two pennies? Yet not one of them is forgotten by God. The hairs of your head are all counted. Do not be afraid, for you are surely as valuable as the sparrows.

Interpreting the Times

When you see a cloud rising in the west, you immediately say, "It is going to rain," and it does. And when you feel the south wind blowing, you say, "There will be scorching heat," and there is. In the evening you say, "Good weather tomorrow," because the sky is red. In the morning you say, "Stormy weather today," because the sky is threatening. You know how to interpret earth and sky. Why is it that you do not know how to interpret the signs of the times?

Faith

If you had faith the size of a mustard seed, you could say to a mulberry tree, "Be uprooted and replanted in the midst of the sea," and the mulberry tree would obey you.

If you had faith the size of a mustard seed, you could say to a mountain, "Move from here to there," and the mountain would move for you.

With faith, all things are possible. If you do not doubt, but believe in your heart that what you say will come to pass, it will be done for you.

Forgiveness

If a person sins against you seven times a day and returns to you repentant seven times, you must forgive that person.

How often should you forgive? Not seven times, but seventy-seven times.

Forgive, and you will be forgiven.

Narrow Gate

Strive to enter through the narrow gate, for many will try and will not be able.

Enter through the narrow gate, for wide is the gate and easy the road that leads to destruction, and there are many who take it.

Narrow the gate that leads to life, and few there are who find it. Hard the road that leads to life, and few there are who take it.

Harvest

Do you not say, "Four months more, and then comes the harvest"? But I tell you, look around you, and see how the fields are ripe for harvesting. The reaper is already receiving wages and is gathering fruit for eternal life, so that sower and reaper may rejoice together. For here the saying holds true, "One sows and another reaps." I sent you to reap what you did not sow, and to harvest that for which you have not labored.

Lesson of the Fig Tree

Look at the fig tree and all the trees. As soon as the branches put forth their leaves, you know that summer is near. So also, when you see certain things taking place, you know that God is near.

This generation will not pass away until all these things have occurred. Heaven and earth will pass away, but my words will not pass away.

Golden Rule

In everything, do to others as you would have them do to you.

Riches

Be on your guard against all kinds of greed, for one's life does not consist in an abundance of possessions.

Where Your Treasure Is

Fear not, little flock, it is God's desire to give you eternal bliss. Sell your possessions and give the money to the poor. Do not store up treasures on earth, where moth consumes and rust destroys and where thieves break in and steal. Provide purses for yourselves that will not wear out and store up an everlasting treasure in heaven. For wherever your treasure is, there will your heart be also.

Greed

No one can serve two authorities. A maidservant will either hate the one and love the other, or be devoted to the one and despise the other. One cannot serve God and greed.

Honesty

Whoever can be trusted in little things can also be trusted in things that are greater. Whoever is dishonest with very little will also be dishonest with much. If you cannot be trusted with material wealth, who will entrust to you genuine riches? If you have not been honest with what belongs to another, how will you manage what is your own?

Worry

Do not worry about tomorrow, for tomorrow will bring worries of its own. Sufficient for today are the troubles of today.

Expectations

Much will be required from the one to whom much has been given; and from the one to whom much has been entrusted, even more will be demanded.

Rest

Come to me, all you who are weary and heavily burdened, and I will give you rest.

Take my yoke upon you, and learn from me; for I am gentle and humble of heart, and you will find rest for your souls. For my yoke is easy, and my burden is light.

Old and New

No one sews a piece of unshrunk cloth on an old garment, for the patch will pull away and the tear will be worse. No one takes a piece from a new garment and sews it on an old one. The new garment will be torn, the new piece will not match the old, and both garments will be ruined. No one puts new wine into old wineskins. The skins will burst, the wine will spill, and everything will be lost. Put new wine into fresh wineskins. Do not mix the old and the new.

Be Who You Are

Be who you are, even as God is who God is.

Wisdom

I will give you words and a wisdom that your opponents will not be able to resist or dare to contradict. Wisdom is vindicated by her deeds and justified by all her children.

IDENTITY OF JESUS

✦

Transfiguration

One day Jesus took Peter and James and John, and went up on the mountain to pray. While he was praying, the men said, his whole being was transfigured: his face shone like the sun and his clothes became dazzling white. Then they saw Moses and Elijah, they said, standing in glory beside him, and they seemed to be talking with him. Now Peter admitted they had been exhausted, and at one point had even fallen asleep, but he knew this vision was real because the three of them had seen it. They were terrified and filled with awe. Peter remembered saying to Jesus, "Rabbi, it is good that we are here. We will build three sanctuaries, for you and Moses and Elijah, right here on this mountain." Then a cloud's shadow covered them, and they heard a voice as if from the cloud, saying, "This is the One I have chosen; listen to him!" They fell to the ground, and when they looked up, they saw only Jesus. He had completed his prayer. They said not a word to anyone until a long time after these strange things had occurred.

Who Do You Say That I Am?

Once when Jesus was alone with his disciples, he asked them, "Who do people say that I am?" They answered,

"Some say John the Baptist, others say Elijah, still others, Jeremiah or one of the other prophets." Then he asked them, "Who do you say that I am?" Mary Magdalene answered, "You are God's Anointed." Peter agreed with her.

Light of the World

Jesus said, "I am the light of the world. All who follow me will be filled with the light of life, and all who believe in me will walk in the light."

Bread of Life

Jesus said, "I am the bread of life. Whoever comes to me will never be hungry; whoever eats of this bread will live forever. I am the living bread that came down from heaven to give life to the world."

True Vine

Jesus said, "I am the true vine; God is the vinegrower who removes barren branches and prunes every fruit-bearing branch so that it might be even more fruitful. As the branch cannot bear fruit by itself unless it abides in the vine, so you cannot be fruitful unless you abide in me. Abide in me as I abide in you. I am the vine, you are the branches. Those who abide in me and I in them will bear much fruit, for apart from me you can do nothing."

Gate

Jesus said, "I am the gate. Whoever enters by me will be saved, and will come in and go out and find green pastures."

Good Shepherd

Jesus said, "I am the good shepherd. I know my own and mine know me. I would lay down my life for my sheep."

Way, Truth, Life

Jesus said, "I am the way, and the truth, and the life."

Living Water

Jesus said, "Ask, and I will give you living water. All you who are thirsty, come to me, all you who believe in me, drink. Whoever believes in me will never thirst again."

DISCIPLESHIP

✦

Following Jesus

As they walked along, a woman approached Jesus and said, "I will follow you wherever you go." Jesus said to her, "Foxes have holes, birds have nests, but those who follow God's Anointed have no such security, for they know not where they will lay their head."

He said to another woman, "Follow me," but she was hesitant and indecisive. "Not while my mother is still alive, for she has need of me," she said. But Jesus replied, "There are others at home who can fulfill that role. Come and proclaim the advent of God."

Another woman said, "I will follow you after my children are grown." Jesus said, for the benefit of all, "Once you have put your hand to the spindle, it is hard to make thread if you keep turning away."

Jesus said to those who would follow him, "If you believe in me, you are my disciples. Hold fast to my word, and you will know the truth, and the truth will set you free. Listen to the wisdom within you, and you will be listening to me."

Cost of Discipleship

At times, men who had joined his company were offended by something Jesus said or did, and they walked away from him. Then Jesus would turn to the women

105

and ask, "Do you also wish to go away?" They would answer, "To whom will we go? Yours are the ways that give us life."

Then Jesus said to his disciples, and to the other women and men who were gathered around him, "Whoever follows me must be willing to make sacrifices and to accept life's trials, whatever they may be. Those who seek security will always be insecure, while those who are willing to risk all security for my sake and for the sake of the gospel will know a deep inner peace. For what value is it if you acquire all that you might humanly desire and yet miss the meaning of life? Whoever follows me must value me above all else — possessions, family bonds, even life itself. That is what I ask of my disciples."

Disciples

To prepare his disciples for ministry, Jesus would often send them ahead, in groups or in pairs, to places where he himself intended to go. Once he sent seventy women with children into the villages and towns, saying: "I am sending you out like lambs among wolves. Carry no purse, no bag, no extra pair of sandals, and do not become distracted on the way. Whatever house you enter, first say, 'Peace to this house!' And if anyone is there who shares that peace, your peace will rest on that person; but if not, it will return to you. Do not move from house to house, but remain in the same house, eating and drinking whatever they provide, for the laborer deserves to be paid. Whenever you enter a town where you are welcome, stay, eat what is set before you, heal those who are sick, and say to them, 'God is very near to you.' But if you enter a town where they do not welcome you, leave not only the town, but even the dust that clings to your sandals, saying, 'Know this: God is very near.'"

The seventy returned to Jesus, rejoicing. "Rabbi, in your name, we were able to do so many things!" Jesus said, "Those who believe in me will continue my work, and will do greater things than these. I have given you authority and power, and I assure you, nothing will hurt you. Yet do not rejoice that the spirits submit to you, but rejoice that your names are written in heaven."

Filled with the Spirit, Jesus gave thanks, saying, "I thank you, God of heaven and earth, that you have hidden certain things from the wise and the intelligent and have revealed them to these little ones, for such was your gracious will."

Then Jesus said to the disciples, "Blessed are the eyes that see what you see! For I tell you that many leaders and prophets desired to see what you see, but did not see it, and to hear what you hear, and did not hear it."

Jesus also selected some of the men, among them Peter and Andrew and James and John and sent them out with similar instructions, saying, "Take no gold, or silver, or copper in your belts, no extra tunic, no bread, no staff." He charged them to proclaim the good news of the nearness of God, saying, "Do not lay down any rules beyond the ones that I have established, and do not make laws like the lawgiver lest you be constrained by them."

Wealthy Woman

Someone came up to Jesus and said, "Teacher, what must I do to have eternal life." Jesus said, "Keep the commandments." She asked, "Which ones?" Jesus replied, "You shall not murder. You shall not commit adultery. You shall not steal. Honor your mother and father." She said, "I have kept these all my life." Jesus said, "Then sell your possessions, give the money to the poor, and come, follow me." When she heard this, she left heavy-hearted, for she was a wealthy woman and she possessed many things. Then Jesus said to his disciples, "How hard it will be for those who have wealth to enter the household of heaven." The disciples were astounded and said, "Then who can be saved?" Jesus looked at them and said, "What seems impossible to you is not impossible to God." Peter said to Jesus, "We have left everything to follow you. What might we expect?" Jesus said, "All who have left home or family or possessions for my sake and for the sake of the good news will receive a hundredfold and will inherit eternal life."

Salome and Her Sons

Salome, mother of James and John, who along with her sons had left their father, Zebedee, to follow Jesus, came to him one day and said, "These two sons of mine continue to argue about who among us will be greatest in heaven. One wants to sit at your right hand, the other wants to sit at your left. Will you grant this favor to them?" Jesus asked, "Will you be faithful to the end?" "Yes," they replied. Jesus said, "To sit at my right hand or at my left is not mine to give. That decision belongs to God." Some of the other men, overhearing this, were angry with the two brothers for seeking an advantage over them. Jesus said to them, "Why do you worry about power and prestige? Whoever seeks such status wishes to prevail over others. This shall not be so with you. The greatest among you must become like the youngest, and the leader like one who serves. I am among you as one who serves."

There were always women with children in the crowds that came to Jesus, and women with children among his disciples. Some of the men found this annoying. The women would often place their infants in the arms of Jesus, or on his lap, and he would cuddle them and bless them. One day when they had paused to rest, some women and children were approaching Jesus when several of the men spoke sternly to them. But Jesus said, "Let the little children come to me. Do not try to stop them, for heaven belongs to such as these." Then looking straight at James and John, he said, "Unless you change and become like children, you will never enter heaven. Whoever becomes like a little child is among the greatest in heaven." Then he took the little ones in his arms, and hugged them, and blessed them.

A Woman in the Crowd

A woman in the crowd raised her voice, saying, "Blessed is the womb that bore you and the breasts that nursed you!" Jesus replied, "Indeed! And blessed are they who hear the word of God and live it, who nurture the wisdom of God and reveal it."

Family of Jesus

As Jesus was speaking to the crowd which had closed in all around him, someone came up to him and said,

"Rabbi, your mother is here. She came with your sisters and brothers. She wants to speak to you." Looking at the people around him, Jesus said, "My mother? My sisters? My brothers? That is who you are to me. Whoever does the will of God is also my mother and sister and brother." Then he got up and went to his mother.

TURNING POINT

✧

John in Prison

Mary, the mother of Jesus, had heard that John had been put in prison. She was worried about Elizabeth's child and concerned about her son, for she feared that he too might become a victim of Herod's wrath.

John had provoked Herod by publicly condemning his marriage to Herodias, his brother's wife. In prison he wrestled with doubts concerning his cousin Jesus. He had begun to question who he really was, so he sent some of his disciples to ask, "Are you the one who is to come, or are we to wait for another?" Jesus replied, "Go tell John what you have seen and heard: the blind see, the lame walk, the deaf hear, the sick are healed, the dead are raised, the poor have good news brought to them. And blessed are the ones who continue to believe in me."

Then Jesus spoke to the crowds about John and his ministry in the wilderness. "What did you go out into the desert to see? A reed shaken by the wind? Really, what did you go out to see? Someone dressed in fine robes? Those who live in luxury are found in palaces. What then did you go out to see? A prophet? Yes, and more than a prophet, for he is the one preparing the way for the One who has been promised."

Death of John

Herod was afraid to put John to death because so many people considered him a prophet. John was languishing in prison when Herod invited his courtiers and officers and his Galilean leaders to a banquet at the palace to celebrate his birthday. Salome, the daughter of Herodias, came in to entertain Herod and his guests, and her dancing charmed them all. Herod said to the girl, "Ask for whatever you wish, and I will give it to you." Then he solemnly swore an oath, repeating, "Whatever you ask, I will give to you, even half my kingdom." The wine had flowed freely that night, and Herod clearly was drunk. The girl went out to her mother and said, "Tell me, what should I ask for?" Herodias replied, "The head of John the baptizer." The girl hurried back to Herod and said, "I want you to give me now, on a platter, the head of John the Baptist." Herod was stunned. He knew he could not refuse her, because all who were present had witnessed his oath. So he gave the order to a soldier of the guard, who went and beheaded John. He returned with the head on a platter, and gave it to the girl, and she gave it to her mother.

When word reached John's disciples, they went and got his body, and laid it in a tomb.

Prophecies and Warnings

John's disciples were devastated. When Jesus learned of the death of his cousin, he grieved at length for him. Many of his followers were frightened; some even feared for his safety. And when he began speaking of the days to come, they wondered if he might be next.

Jesus said to his disciples, "The days are coming when

you will long for deliverance, and you will not experience it. There will be sacrilege in sacred places. The love of many will grow cold. Do not be led astray, for many will speak in my name, saying, 'I am God's Anointed.' False messiahs and false prophets will appear and produce great signs and omens, to lead astray, if possible, even the elect. For as a flash of lightning lights up the sky from one side to the other, so also will God's Anointed. But first must come the suffering. You will hear of wars and rumors of wars. Nation will rise against nation, and there will be earthquakes and famines. All this is but the beginning of the birthpangs.

"Be vigilant, for you know neither the day nor the hour. On that night, there will be two in one bed; one will be taken and the other left. There will be two women grinding meal together; one will be taken and the other left. Those in Judea must flee to the mountains. The one on the housetop must not go down to take what is in the house; the one in the field must not go back to get a shawl or a coat. Woe to those who are pregnant and to those who are nursing infants! Pray that it not be in winter. There will be great suffering, greater than any experienced since the beginning of the world.

"Immediately after those days, the sun will grow dark, the moon will lose its light, the stars will fall from heaven, and all the earth will mourn. God will come, riding the clouds, with power and with glory, and will gather the elect from the four winds, and from one end of time to the other. Yes, God is coming; yet the truth is, God is already here among you."

Jesus spoke of the persecutions to come and the suffering which awaited his disciples. "As for you, my followers, be prepared! For they will hand you over to the powers that prevail. You will be brought before the authorities, those governing religion and those that rule the world, and you will be mistreated, and you will be judged. When they bring you to trial, do not worry beforehand about what you are to say; but say whatever is given you at that time, for the Spirit will speak through you. You will be hated because of my name, but endure to the end and you will be saved."

Return to Nazareth

Jesus returned to Nazareth and began to teach in the synagogue. People were impressed. "Where did this man get his wisdom?" they asked. "Isn't he the carpenter's son? Isn't his mother called Mary? Are not his sisters here among us? Are not his brothers James and Joseph and Simon and Judas? Then where did he get all this?" Some, however, were offended at his words. Others were envious. Jesus said, "Prophets are not without honor except in their own country and in their own house." And he did very little in Nazareth because of their lack of belief.

One sabbath day, Jesus was there in the synagogue expounding on the scripture. He said, "Doubtless you will quote to me this proverb, 'Doctor, cure yourself!' And you will say, 'Do here in your hometown what they say you have done in Capernaum.'" And again he said, "Truly I tell you, prophets are not accepted in their own hometown. There were many widows in Israel during the time of severe famine, yet Elijah was sent only to a widow at Zarephath, which is in Sidon. And there were many with leprosy in Israel, and none were healed except Naaman of Syria."

When they heard this, the men were filled with rage. He had spoken in favor of women and those who had leprosy; he had preached salvation for foreigners; he had rejected God's chosen people. They drove him out of town and were pushing him toward the brow of the hill so that they might hurl him over the cliff, but his brothers helped him slip away. Then under cover of darkness, with the aid of his sisters and brothers, he made it to the outskirts of Nazareth, where he joined with several disciples and continued on his way.

Passing through Samaria

Jesus journeyed through Samaria on his way to Jerusalem. Several disciples had gone ahead to prepare the way for him. They entered a Samaritan village and said that Jesus was approaching, but the people refused to receive him. On hearing this, James and John wanted to burn the village down. Jesus had to restrain them as they walked to a village further on.

RETURN TO JERUSALEM

✦

Zaccheus

As Jesus was passing through Jericho, a man named Zaccheus was determined to catch a glimpse of him, for the women of his household seemed to talk of no one else. Since he could not push his way through the crowd, and he could not see from where he stood because most other men were taller than he was, he ran on ahead, climbed a sycamore tree, and watched as Jesus approached. Jesus looked up and saw him and said, "Zaccheus, come down. I would like to stay at your house today." Zaccheus knew his wife would be pleased, and he himself felt honored, but some in the crowd were critical, saying, "He has chosen to be the guest of a sinner." Hearing this, Zaccheus said to Jesus, "Sir, half my possessions I will give to the poor; and if I have cheated anyone of anything, I will pay them back fourfold." He begged him to come to his house; and Jesus went home with him.

Jesus Enters Jerusalem

Jesus left Jericho and went up to Jerusalem. As he drew near the city, crowds came out to meet him, people who had come up for the festival from Galilee and throughout Judea where they had witnessed his charismatic ministry. Many inhabitants of Jerusalem rejoiced at his return. Women with their children pressed close to him. Someone gave him a donkey to ride, for the ascent to the city had been long and hot and draining, and he seemed tired. Dancing, singing psalms of praise, spontaneously waving branches of palm, they escorted him into Jerusalem with festive celebration in an impromptu street parade.

Jesus Weeps over Jerusalem

When he was alone in a quiet place on a hill overlooking the city, Jesus was moved to tears and lamented, "Jerusalem, Jerusalem, city that kills the prophets and stones those who are sent to you! How I have longed to gather your children together as a hen gathers her brood safely and tenderly under her wings, but you were never willing! Now your house will be left desolate. For I tell you, you will not see me again until the time comes when you will say, 'Blessed is the one who comes in the name of God.'"

Poor Widow

Jesus sat watching people put money in the temple treasury. The rich were usually generous. When he saw a poor widow give two small coins, he turned to his disciples and said, "This poor widow's gift is worth far more than all other contributions, for they gave of their abundance from the money they had left over, while she gave all the money she had from the little she had to live on."

Money Changers in the Temple

Then he entered the temple and was deeply disturbed by the chaos caused by the buyers and sellers engaged in commercial exchange, and the hypocrisy of the money changers who exploited and cheated the poor. He overturned one of the tables, saying, "This temple is a house of prayer, but you have made it a den of thieves." They were angry enough to kill him, but many people were deeply moved by what they had seen and heard. Jesus left the temple and went to the home of his friends in Bethany, where he was staying during the festival. Martha and Mary listened for hours as he poured out his heart to them.

Paying Taxes

After the temple incident, the religious authorities were looking for a way to entrap Jesus with his own words, so that they might hand him over to the civil authorities for punishment. They sent representatives who asked him, "Rabbi, we know you teach God's ways; but tell us, is it lawful for us to pay taxes to Caesar, or not?" Jesus said, "Show me a coin. Whose image and title are on it?" They said, "The emperor Caesar's." Jesus said, "Then give to Caesar the things that are Caesar's, and to God the things that are God's." The cleverness of his answer stunned them into silence, and once again he slipped away.

LAST DAYS

✧

A Woman Anoints Jesus

Jesus was in Bethany at the house of Simon, an outcast, when a woman with an alabaster jar of very costly ointment came up to him as he sat at the table. She poured the ointment over his head. Some who were present were furious. "Let her alone," said Jesus. "She dared to do what she has done because she has recognized me. Truly I say to you, whenever this good news is proclaimed anywhere in the world, what she has done in memory of me will be told in memory of her."

Plot to Kill Jesus

As the Passover festival approached, the chief priests and the elders of the people were looking for a way to put Jesus to death. They feared his popularity, which was a threat to religious security, for he was leading many astray by ignoring tradition and the law. They had reached the end of their endurance with his blasphemous behavior and his flagrant violation of their rituals and their rules. Reports were pouring in from all over Judea and Galilee. He had healed people on the sabbath, had picked grain on the sabbath, had declared himself above the sabbath, saying, "The sabbath was made for people, and not people for the sabbath." He had even blasphemed the temple,

119

talked of its destruction, saying, "Not a single stone upon a stone will be left of all its splendor."

If they were going to arrest Jesus, they would have to do it quietly. "Not during the festival," they said, "or there will be a riot among the people." Then they thought of a way to get to him. One who was part of his inner circle was a hypocrite and a thief. They felt certain they could bribe him to deliver Jesus to them.

Some officials found an opportunity to confer with Judas Iscariot. The promise of a fistful of silver was enough to gain his consent. Judas agreed to betray him.

On Death and Resurrection

When Jesus was alone with his disciples, he said quietly to them, "I will be betrayed into human hands. They are going to kill me; but I will rise again." They did not understand his words, but they were afraid to question him. A premonition of dread gripped the heart of Mary Magdalene. Martha came and sat beside him, and silently held his hand.

Hypocrites and Hypocrisy

During the days prior to the festival, Jesus was constantly badgered by those who were trying to trip him up. Exasperated, he delivered a stinging rebuke against religious hypocrites and their hypocrisy.

"Woe to you, religious leaders, who do not practice what you teach; who dole out heavy burdens, never offering to alleviate them; who live to be seen by others; who love places of honor and to be greeted with respect.

"Woe to you, religious authorities, who do everything in your power to make heaven inaccessible to those entrusted to you.

"Woe to you, religious hypocrites, who worry about trivial tithes and ignore justice and mercy, causing many to fall from faith.

"Woe to you, religious guides, who carefully polish the outside, but inside are full of self-indulgent greed. You may impress others, but God knows you are white-washed tombs.

"Woe to you who bury the prophets and persecute the just.

"Woe to you who are rich through a selfish accumulation of riches; for you have received your consolation.

"Woe to you who are full now, for you will hunger for food.

"Woe to you who are laughing now, for you will mourn and weep.

"Woe to you who reject God's commandments in order to hold on to your tradition, who teach human precepts as though they were doctrines of God.

"Woe to you who pray with your lips, but whose hearts are far from God, for your worship is in vain."

Judgement of the Nations

"On that day, when all the nations of the earth are assembled to hear the word of judgement and the call to eternal glory, the Holy One will look with love on all who lived with justice and mercy, saying,

"'Come, blessed, receive the bliss awaiting you from the beginning; for I was hungry and you gave me food; I was thirsty and you gave me drink; I was a stranger and you welcomed me; I was naked and you clothed me; I was sick and you took care of me; I was in prison and you visited me.' Then the blessed will answer,

"'O Holy One, when did we see you hungry and feed you, or thirsty, and give you something to drink? Or when did we welcome you, a stranger, or see you naked and give you clothes? Or when did we see you sick or in prison, and care for you, and comfort you?' And the Holy One will say to them,

"'Truly, whenever you reached out in love to any of mine who were in need, or gave of yourself to those labeled least important, you reached out in love to me.' Then the Holy One will say,

"'Woe to you who have yet to accomplish what God is asking of you; for I was hungry and you gave me nothing to eat; I was thirsty and you gave me nothing to drink; I was a stranger and you did not welcome me, naked and you did not clothe me, sick and you did not care for me; in prison and you did not come to comfort me.' Then those astounded ones will reply,

"'When did we see you hungry or thirsty, or a stranger, or naked, or sick, or in prison, and not reach out to you?' Then the Holy One will answer,

"'Whenever you withheld compassion, or justice, or mercy, whenever you refused to give of yourself to those you labeled least important or failed to reach out in love to any of mine who were in need, you failed to reach out to me.'

"Then the feeling of loss will be so severe that no external punishment could compare to the suffering endured by those who one day realize they failed to live according to the law of love."

PASSION NARRATIVE BEGINS

Passover Meal

On the first day of Unleavened Bread, some of the disciples asked Jesus, "Where will we eat our Passover meal?" Jesus said, "One of the women has offered us a large upper room in her home in the city, one that is already furnished. Some of our women have been there since early morning, making preparations." They went into the city to where Jesus had said and found everything just as he had told them. Martha was busy preparing the food, her sister was arranging candles and cloths, and the Galilean women were assisting them.

When evening came, Jesus took his place among his family and friends. His mother and her sister sat with the sisters and cousins of Jesus; his brothers joined the other men. Mary Magdalene, Mary the mother of James and Joseph, Salome, Joanna, Susanna, and all the women who had come up from Galilee sat among the women from Bethany and Jerusalem and the Judean countryside.

Peter and James and John managed to get places close to Jesus, John to the right of Jesus, with Peter next to him. Jesus had overheard them bickering about seniority and rank, so when the women who were serving came in with basins of water for washing, he got up from the table, took a basin and towel from one of the women, and began to wash their feet. He came to Peter, who vigorously protested, saying, "You will never wash my feet!" Jesus replied, "Someday you will know and understand what I have been trying to teach you." Then he proceeded to wash Peter's feet. When he was finished, he said, "Do you see what I am doing? I am setting an example. Do as I have done. Love one another as I have loved you."

When he had taken his place again at table, he took bread, blessed it, broke it, and gave it to them saying, "Take, eat." Then looking at each of them with love, he spoke about how they were now all one body in a covenant of love. He called upon God and prayed, "that they may be one as we are one, I in them and you in me, that they may be truly one." The women hung on his every word. After the meal, he took the cup of wine, and when he had given thanks, he gave it to them, saying, "Take, drink." He spoke of a new covenant as he compared the cup of wine to "my blood poured out for you."

A feeling of anguish came over his mother as she heard him speak those words. The women all fell silent. The men were confused about what he had said. Then Jesus said to the men who were sitting near him at table, "And one of you will betray me." Horrified, they began to ask, "Who is it? Surely, not I?" Jesus looked at Judas; Judas got up and left the room.

After they had sung the final hymn, Jesus spoke again to the men who were sitting closest to him. "Tonight, you will all desert me." Again the men were horrified, and all of them protested. Peter said defiantly, "Even if all of these become deserters, I will never desert you."

Then Jesus said to Peter, "This very night, before the cock crows twice, three times you will deny me." Peter argued vehemently. "Even if it means I die with you, I will not deny you." All of them said the same. They would go to prison, and if need be, they would go to their death with him.

Gethsemane

It was late when Jesus left the upper room. The women remained to put things in order before retiring for the night. Jesus was going to the Mount of Olives to pray quietly in a garden there; he felt a need for silence and solitude. Stung by his accusations, the men were determined not to let him out of their sight, so they went along with him.

When they reached the garden of Gethsemane, Jesus withdrew about a stone's throw from them and experienced an agony of spirit. He prayed that God would remove his terror, that the danger he sensed might pass, yet prayed, "not my will but yours be done." After some time, he returned to the others, and found them fast asleep. He looked at them with affection. The night had been long, the wine and food had been plentiful, he had drained them emotionally. "So you would die with me," he mused, "yet here you are, asleep. You could not even watch one hour with me. The spirit indeed is willing, but the flesh is weak." Then he woke them, saying, "Get up. It is time for us to be going."

PASSION AND DEATH
OF JESUS

✧

Betrayal and Arrest of Jesus

As they were leaving the garden, they were stopped by a crowd carrying clubs and swords. It had been organized by the chief priests and elders, and Judas was among them. He had said, "The one I kiss is the one you want." Seeing Jesus, he said to him, "Rabbi!" then walked up to him and kissed him. The mob grabbed Jesus and arrested him. But one of the disciples drew out a sword and cut off the ear of the high priest's slave. The mob went after the disciples of Jesus with weapons and with clubs, and every one of them fled. Jesus said to the unruly mob, "You have come to arrest me with swords and clubs as though I were a bandit. I sat daily in the temple teaching. Why did you not arrest me then?"

Jesus before the Council

Jesus was taken to the house of Caiaphas the high priest, where the scribes and elders had gathered. Peter followed at a distance, then slipped into the courtyard of the high priest's house, where he blended in with the crowd. Inside, the chief priests and the whole council were holding an interrogation. They were seeking false testimony against Jesus so that they might put him to death, but they could find nothing substantial among the many witnesses that came forward. Through it all, Jesus was silent. At last the high priest said to him, "Tell us, are you God's Anointed?" Jesus said, "Yes, I am." That was all they needed. The high priest tore his garments and said, "Why are we looking for witnesses? We have all heard his blasphemy. What is the council's verdict?" They said he should be put to death.

Through the rest of the night, the soldiers who guarded him spit on him, beat him, insulted him, and mocked him mercilessly.

High Priest's Maid

One of the maids of the high priest saw Peter in the courtyard, warming himself by the fire. She stared at him for a moment, then said, "You were also with Jesus the Galilean." But Peter vehemently denied it, saying, "I have no idea what you mean." Later, she saw him again on the porch, and she said to the bystanders, "This man is one of them." But again, Peter denied it, saying, "I do not know the man." Eventually the bystanders said to Peter, "Surely you are one of their company, for your accent is Galilean." He began to curse, then he swore with an oath, "I do not know the man!" At that moment, he heard a cock crow, and Peter remembered Jesus saying that he would deny him three times. He went into the night, weeping bitterly. The maid went into the house disillusioned. She had overheard what was being said about Jesus, about his teachings, his marvelous deeds. She had thought his followers would surely be willing to die for such a man. She felt sorry for him.

At first light, the chief priests and the elders of the people led Jesus, bound, to Pilate the governor so that he might condemn him to death. They listed their accusations against him. Pilate asked Jesus, "Are you the king of the Jews?" Jesus said, "It is you saying this, not I." He did not answer any more questions, nor did he respond to any charges. "Do you not hear how many accusations they are making against you?" Pilate asked. "They are saying that you are leading women and children astray." But Jesus stood silent before him.

While he was sitting in judgement on Jesus, Pilate's wife sent a message to her husband. "Have nothing to do with that innocent man. I have been upset all day because of a dream I had about him." Her comment troubled Pilate. Now at festival time it was customary for the governor to release a prisoner to the people, anyone they wanted. There was in custody at the time a criminal called Barabbas. When the crowd assembled, Pilate asked them, "Whom do you want me to release to you, Jesus or Barabbas?" He felt certain the crowd would ask for Jesus, but the chief priests and the elders persuaded the people to call for Barabbas. Pilate asked again, "Which of the two shall I release to you?" The crowd cried out, "Barabbas!" Dismayed, Pilate responded, "And what shall I do with Jesus?" They cried out, "Crucify him!" Pilate asked, "Why? What evil has he done?" But they shouted even louder, "Let him be crucified!" Pilate felt that Jesus had done nothing deserving of death. But he saw that it was futile, that the crowd was getting out of control. So he took some water and washed his hands in full view of those assembled, saying, "I am innocent of this man's blood. The responsibility is yours." Then he released Barabbas, had Jesus scourged, and ordered his crucifixion. Pilate's wife went into seclusion and was never the same again.

Daughters of Jerusalem

The governor's soldiers stripped Jesus, gave him a crown of thorns, and jeered him, saying, "Hail, king of the Jews!" Then they led him away to be crucified. Because Jesus was already weak, they forced a man who was a visitor in the city to carry his cross for him. A crowd of people followed him, among them women who beat their breasts, women weeping and wailing. Jesus turned to them and said, "Daughters of Jerusalem, do not weep for me, but weep for yourselves and for your children, especially your daughters. For the days are coming when people will say, 'Blessed are those who are childless; blessed are the wombs that have never given birth and the breasts that have never nursed.'"

Crucifixion

When they came to the place which is called The Skull, they crucified Jesus, and with him two criminals, one on the right and one on the left; and they cast lots for his garments. Many stood by silently, watching. Others mocked him, saying, "He saved others, but he cannot save himself," and "If you are really the Messiah, then come down from that cross!" Quite close to the cross stood Mary, his mother. Who on earth can comprehend her agony at that hour. Grieving beside her were her sister, and Mary Magdalene, and Mary who was married to Cleopas. Close behind them, clinging to one another for comfort and support, were the sisters and cousins of Jesus, Mary and Martha of Bethany, Mary the mother of James and Joseph, Salome and all the Galilean women who had come up to Jerusalem, the women of Jerusalem who had wept for him as he followed the cross to his death, and many village women who had come into the city from the Judean countryside. At the back of the crowd, heavily veiled, stood the high priest's maid. Behind her was Pilate's wife. Peter and the other male disciples were nowhere to be found. Seeing Mary Magdalene beside his mother, Jesus looked from one to the other. His beloved disciple understood. From then on, she and the Galilean women would be family to the mother of Jesus, supporting her with their love.

Death of Jesus

From midday until three in the afternoon, the sky grew dark and an uneasiness gripped the hearts of many. At about three o'clock, Jesus cried out in a loud voice, *"Eli, eli, lema sabachthani?"* ... "My God, my God, why have you forsaken me?" He cried out again, and breathed his last.

Burial of Jesus

A man named Joseph from the Jewish town of Arimathea helped the women take the body of Jesus down from the cross, and they placed him in the arms of his mother. She held him close, grieving for the precious child of her womb as all the women wept with her.

Joseph had gone to Pilate for permission to bury the body of Jesus, and Pilate had granted his request. Although he was a member of the council, Joseph had not participated in the condemnation of Jesus. When the soldiers were satisfied that Jesus was dead, the women wrapped his body in the new linen cloth which Joseph had provided. Then they carried the body to the burial place, a new tomb in a rock; and Joseph rolled a stone in front of the opening to the tomb. Many of the women remained there. They had arranged among themselves how they would take turns at the tomb, keeping vigil throughout the sabbath, waiting until they could anoint his body properly for burial.

HE IS RISEN!

✧

Resurrection

In the pre-dawn stillness, Mary looked through sleepless eyes at the all-encompassing night. Sitting quietly beside the window, she felt before she saw the familiar presence she so loved. "Mother," said Jesus softly, as a radiance enfolded her, filling her with light. She was a young girl again. The Spirit of God was in her, and she felt the familiar stirrings of life in the hollow deep inside.

When he had gone, Mary sat for a long time, cherishing him in her heart. Then she rose and went to her sister, and together they told their daughters, and their sorrow was as nothing compared to their joy.

Jesus Appears to Mary Magdalene

It was still dark in the early morning hours after the sabbath. Mary Magdalene sat near the tomb, weeping. As dawn broke, she looked up and saw that the stone had been rolled away. How could that have happened? Had she fallen asleep? Had they taken him away during her watch? Suddenly, she heard a voice beside her, "Woman, why are you weeping?" Startled, she turned and saw a man whom she thought must be the gardener. "They have taken away my loved one, and I do not know where they have laid him." Then Jesus said to her, "Mary!" She responded in awe, *Rabbouni!* (Teacher!)

Eventually, Jesus spoke again. "You cannot hold on to me. I must return to the One Who sent me." He told her to tell the others. She ran from the garden elated and carried the news to the women. "He is risen! I have seen him!" she said. His mother and sisters, and Martha and Mary, said they already knew. Then she went to tell the men, but they thought she must have been dreaming. None of them believed her. She searched the city for Peter, but he and James and a number of the others were nowhere to be found.

Jesus Appears to the Women

The sabbath was over, and Salome, Susanna, Joanna, and Mary the mother of James and Joseph were returning to the tomb with spices. The other women would be joining them there to anoint the body of Jesus. They wondered if all of them together could roll the stone aside. But when they reached the tomb, they saw that the stone had been removed. And then they saw a vision of Jesus, radiant with light. "Do not be afraid," he said to them, and their terror turned to joy. "Go tell the brothers I have risen from the dead. Say that I have gone to Galilee, and that I will see them there." Then they ran through the city to tell the others about what had just occurred.

On the Road to Emmaus

Later that day, two of the disciples were returning to the village of Emmaus, which was seven miles from Jerusalem, grieving over all that had happened. As Mary and her husband, Cleopas, were walking, Jesus approached and walked along with them, but they failed to recognize him. "What are you discussing?" he asked. Cleopas replied, "You must be the only one in Jerusalem who is unaware of all the things that have happened there these days." Jesus asked, "What things?" and they told him. "The tragedy of Jesus of Nazareth," said Cleopas, "a prophet mighty in word and deed before God and all the people. Our religious leaders wanted him dead, so they had him crucified. We had hoped that he would be the one to liberate Israel." Mary said, "But that is not all. This morning some of our women went to the tomb to anoint his body and found that he was gone. They said they had seen a vision. It was Jesus. He was alive." Her husband, Cleopas, continued. "Some of us went at once to the tomb and found it just as the women had said, but we did not see Jesus. It must have been a vision of angels." Then Jesus said, "Oh, foolish men! How slow of heart you are to believe all that these prophets have spoken!"

As they drew near to the village, Jesus appeared to be journeying on, but they begged him to remain with them. "Come and spend the night with us, for the day is nearly over," they said. Now while he was with them at table, he took the bread and said the blessing, then broke it and gave it to them. Suddenly, their eyes were opened, and they recognized him; but he vanished from their sight. Overjoyed, they said to one another, "Were our hearts not burning within us as he talked to us on the road?" They returned at once to Jerusalem to where the mother of Jesus was staying, arriving quite late at night. Many of the disciples were gathered there. "He is risen!" someone shouted. Then they told them about what had happened to them, and how they had recognized Jesus in the breaking of the bread.

Peter had gone to Galilee. He had left Jerusalem the very night of his humiliation. Overcome with shame and remorse, he had gone back to the sea, unable to face anyone who had been part of that other life. As the disciples began returning home, some of them sought him out. The women said they had seen Jesus. They said that he was alive. But Peter did not believe them. Jesus was dead. This painful fact Peter could not deny.

One afternoon, James and John and some of the others were walking by the sea. They called to Peter, but he turned away, saying, "I am going fishing." They said, "We will go with you." They got into the boat and went out on the lake, but that night they caught nothing.

Shortly after daybreak, they saw someone standing on the beach, but they did not know it was Jesus. "Friends," Jesus called out to them, "have you caught any fish?" They answered, "No! We have nothing." Then he said, "Cast your net to the right of the boat." They did, and they caught so many fish they could barely haul the net in. John said to Peter, "It is Jesus!" Peter paid no attention to him. Instead, he jumped into the sea — they were only about a hundred yards from land — and began pulling the net ashore. The other disciples brought the boat in, dragging their net full of fish.

When they had gone ashore, they saw Jesus tending a charcoal fire. Jesus called over to Peter. "Bring some of the fish you just caught." Peter did, then went back to help with the net, for their catch was exceedingly large both in number and in size. Then Jesus called out to the disciples, "Come and have some breakfast," and he served them bread and fish. None of them dared to ask, "Who are you?" for they knew that it was Jesus.

Jesus and Peter

When they had finished eating, Jesus took Peter aside and said, "Peter, do you love me?" Out of the depths of his anguish, Peter cried, "Yes! I really love you!" Jesus said, "I know, Peter; I know that you love me." Jesus asked a second question. "Peter, do you know that I love you?" Peter hesitated, looked at Jesus, then said, "Yes, I know that you love me." Jesus said, "Forgive yourself, for I have forgiven you." Then he asked a third question. "Peter, can you love yourself as I have loved you?" Relieved of his crushing burden of guilt, Peter broke down and wept, saying, "Help me to learn to love myself as much as I love you."

Then Jesus told Peter that to be a leader meant there would be times when he too would be led. "Before," said Jesus, "you did what you wished; but now others will take you where you do not want to go." Jesus told him to support his lambs. He meant, accept the women. Affirm them, listen to them, and above all, believe them. "Together, tend to the flock," said Jesus. "Come now, follow me."

Jesus in Jerusalem

Peter gathered the Galilean disciples, and together they returned to Jerusalem, the women along with the men. They went back to the upper room, and made that their meeting place. One day, while they were there in that place, Jesus appeared among them and said, "Peace be with you." Those who had not yet seen him were startled and terrified, for they thought they were seeing a ghost. Jesus said to them, "Why are you so frightened, and why do doubts arise in your hearts? I tell you, it is really me."

Thomas had not been present when Jesus appeared in their midst, for he had not returned to their fellowship. After the loss of their leader, he had felt it was pointless to continue on. The other disciples went to him, insisting, "We have seen him. He is alive!" But Thomas said, "Unless I see the mark of the nails in his hand, and put my finger on the wound of the nails, I will not believe."

The following week the disciples were together again in the upper room. Peter had spoken at length with Thomas, and he had agreed to join them. The doors were locked, for they lived in fear of imprisonment and death. Suddenly, Jesus was there among them. "Peace be with you," he said. Then Jesus turned to Thomas. "Come, put your finger here, into the wounds of my hands. Do not doubt any longer, but believe!" Thomas cried, "I believe!" And Jesus said to Thomas, "You believe because you have seen for yourself. Blessed are those who have not seen and still have believed."

LIVING IN THE SPIRIT

✧

Ascension

Jesus was in Bethany at the home of Martha and Mary. All the women were there. His mother was among them. He had said the time was coming when he would no longer be visible to them; and so the community gathered wherever he appeared.

The men eventually joined them, wondering if they were to observe the sabbath in Bethany instead of Jerusalem. But Jesus led them back to the city and then to the Mount of Olives; he spoke his final words to them there.

He said, "For this little while you have seen me, but in a little while, you will see me no more." And they were saddened and dismayed. "Do not let your hearts be troubled," he said, "for I go to prepare a place for you; and in a little while, you will see me again." He said, "I have many things still to say to you, but you cannot bear them now. But my Spirit will speak my words to you and will guide you in the truth." Then he looked directly at the women and said, "You are witnesses. Tell of all you have seen and heard. God's Spirit will fill you, and you will receive the power to be my witnesses, not only in Jerusalem, but throughout Judea and Samaria, and even to the ends of the earth." Then suddenly, he was gone; and in their hearts each one of them knew they would never see him in this way again.

They all returned to Jerusalem, a sabbath walk away, and entered the room where they had been staying. They were Mary, the mother of Jesus, her sister and his sisters, his cousins and relatives; Mary Magdalene; Mary and Martha of Bethany; Mary with her husband, Cleopas; Mary the mother of James and Joseph; Salome, Susanna, Joanna, and the other Galilean women; the widow from Nain, who was there with her son; the wife of Jairus and her daughter; the Canaanite woman and her daughter; the Samaritan woman from Sychar; Peter's wife and mother-in-law; Philip's four daughters; and other wives and daughters. There were also many women from Jerusalem and the Judean countryside: Mary the mother of John Mark with her daughter and her granddaughter, and Rhoda who was her maid; Tabitha and the widows from Jaffa; women who had been healed or touched by Jesus, among them, the woman who had been saved from stoning, the woman healed of the flow of blood, the woman healed of a crippling condition, the two who had anointed Jesus, some widows and other daughters of Jerusalem. In the room were also the men, among them, the brothers and cousins of Jesus, Peter and the sons of Salome and their Galilean companions, and the brother of Martha and Mary.

They were all together in prayer as the day of Pentecost dawned, when suddenly a sound like the sound of wind shook the room where they were praying, and the hearts of all of them burned like fire. Filled with the power of the Spirit, their fears and inhibitions fell away, and they went out into the streets of Jerusalem, singing and praising God. They stopped all who were passing by to preach God's word to them. Visitors from distant cities and many Jews from Jerusalem were astonished as they heard the good news preached in words they could understand. Some said to one another, "How can this be, for even the women are making sense to us; yes, and even their servants," for some recognized the maids. To the skeptical, Peter responded, "This was predicted by the prophet Joel who wrote:

> 'In those days, God promised,
> I will pour out my Spirit upon all flesh,
> and your daughters and sons shall prophesy:
> the young will have vision,
> the old will dream dreams.
> Even upon slaves, both women and men,
> I will pour out my Spirit;
> and they too shall prophesy.'

And all who hear their word and believe will belong to the household of God."

EPILOGUE

✧

Now Jesus did many other things for and with women, but the whole of our tradition could not be written down, for it would fill too many books. These things have been recorded here so that women may take heart in knowing how it was for us, and knowing, might believe.

The Gospel According to Mary *took flesh on the rim of the Kalahari desert, a section of southern Africa reminiscent of the homeland of Jesus with its desert sand and stone made in the image of the Judean wilderness, its village wells and village life, its dirt roads and sparse vegetation, its sheep and goats and shepherds, its donkey carts and uncluttered climate transcending the boundaries of time and space, integrating then and now. I give thanks to Her Who led me here to drink deep of Her Spirit and to be blessed by all that is sacred beneath the stars of the southern cross. May we make peace with the possibility of a gospel written by a woman, so that one day, when we find one, we will not be too surprised.*

Mahalapye, Botswana
May 1992